KEYS TO PARENTING YOUR TEENAGER

KEYS TO PARENTING YOUR TEENAGER

SECOND EDITION

DON FONTENELLE

SELFHELP SUCCESS BOOKS

Gretna 2012

First published by Barron's Educational Series, Inc.,1992
Published by arrangement with the author by
    Selfhelp Success Books, L.L.C., 2012

First edition, 1992
Second edition, 2000
First Selfhelp Success edition, 2012

Selfhelp Success, Selfhelp Success Books, and
are imprints of Selfhelp Success Books, L.L.C.

Library of Congress Cataloging-in-Publication Data

Fontenelle, Don, 1946-
    Keys to parenting your teenager / Don H. Fontenelle
        p.   cm.
    Includes bibliographical references and index.
    ISBN 978-1-93523-508-8 (pbk. : alk. paper) ; 978-1-93523-509-5 (e-book)
    1. Parent and teenager—United States. 2. Adolescent
psychology—United States. I. Title. II. Series.
  HQ799.15.F66   2000
  649.125—dc21   00-031148
                                                        CIP

Printed in the United States of America
Published by Selfhelp Success Books, L.L.C.
900 Burmaster Street, Gretna, Louisiana 70053

CONTENTS

INTRODUCTION

Many times when my children were younger and I took them fishing with their friends, or when we went someplace with other children, they would say, "Dad, tell Preston and Glenn about the old times. Tell them what the price of a Coke was and how much it cost to go to a movie. Tell them how many fish you used to catch in Bayou Bienvenue."

Needless to say, there have been significant changes since the "olden days" when you and I—now the parents of teenagers—were adolescents. Many of these changes have made adolescence a more difficult time for children—and parents.

In the late '50s and early '60s, a survey showed that adolescents ranked parents as the most influential people in their lives, with the other top ten choices also authority figures (e.g., teachers, coaches, political figures, the president). A recent survey ranked parents ninth—the only authority figures in the top ten. The other nine were sports figures, movie stars, singers, and other entertainment celebrities.

In the '40s and early '50s, the leading disciplinary problems in school, according to teachers, were talking, chewing gum, making noise, and getting out of place in line. The current concerns are drug and alcohol abuse, pregnancy, suicide, rape, robbery, assault, burglary, arson, guns, shootings, and bombings—a much more frightening lineup.

Divorce, single parenting, and stepparenting have significantly increased. In many families both parents work, and children are spending more time in before- and after-school care facilities or on their own. Drugs are readily available. Movies and TV provide children with information about complex life experiences at very young ages. In general, life moves at a faster pace.

Adolescence in and of itself is a period of change for the child and for parents. We're no longer dealing with a child but an emerging young adult. Therefore, methods of discipline, interaction, communication, and control must change. Parents need to become aware of normal teenage behaviors to deal effectively with the adolescent on a daily basis. Often I see parents having trouble with their teenager because they still use management techniques they used when the child was younger.

This book was written to help parents deal with adolescents who are showing normal healthy development. It is not about teenagers with gross emotional disturbance or serious behavior disorders or those who are completely "out of control." More intense interventions or professional help is necessary in these situations.

This book is designed to give you a better understanding of your adolescent and more effective methods to interact with the child on a day-to-day basis. Use of the techniques and concepts presented should make your household run more smoothly and reduce the conflicts you experience in your daily interaction. I have purposefully avoided psychological terminology, discussion of theory, and abstract concepts. Using everyday language, I have presented the concepts in a practical, down-to-earth manner with numerous examples. This should make the book easy to read and understand.

1

TYPICAL TEENAGE BEHAVIORS AND ATTITUDES

Most of the information written about adolescents and teenagers places a great deal of emphasis on the physical, social, and emotional changes, accompanied by confusion and uncertainty, that mark this developmental stage of a child's life. While it is certainly a difficult period for the child, it is likewise true that the parents are also experiencing stresses, changes, and confusion at this time. Not much has been written about the parents' problems and worries, as well as the changes they are undergoing as they approach midlife with a teenager in their household.

It is important to recognize some of the normal behaviors and reactions of parents and teens during this period. Many parents perceive certain teen attitudes and behaviors to be problems, whereas in reality these may follow typical adolescent patterns and should be dealt with as such.

Following are some suggestions on how to distinguish between normal and abnormal behavior in an adolescent and how to decide whether the behavior should be of no concern, or of mild, moderate, or great concern to the parent.

What Is Normal? How moody should a child be? How talkative, rebellious, oppositional, or resistant? What is normal teenage behavior? These questions are difficult to answer specifically. In general, normal behavior is that behavior that does not interfere with a person's ability to cope with his environment or to get along with others. It is relatively easy to find a child-development book that will tell you at what age a child should walk, talk, or get his or her first tooth. Other books will tell you what to expect at certain ages (e.g., the terrible twos). But just how do you determine what is a normal amount of flippancy or moodiness in your teenager? In trying to decide what is typical, there are several factors to consider.

Become Aware of the Attitudes and Behaviors of Adolescents Your Child's Age. I am not recommending that you keep up with the Joneses or go along with the crowd. However, you must consider your teenager's peer group and take into account the behaviors and actions of his age mates in order to determine if your teenager's behavior is typical or should be of concern. In other words, you have to compare your child with other children his age. Talk to other parents with teenagers. Observe your child's friends and other similar-age children.

The child's peer groups—their behaviors, attitudes, dress, values—must be taken into consideration before deciding what is normal for your child. But, you also must try to determine what the "normal" peer groups are. Some peer groups are in themselves deviant and may be associated with serious impairments or difficulties.

Teachers, coaches, tutors, dance instructors, school counselors, and others who work with teenagers are usually familiar with age-appropriate or normal behavior. Although they may not be able to give reasons for certain behavior or recommendations for dealing with it, they can identify actions differing from those of the child's age group.

How Often Does the Behavior Occur? All children, at one time or another, are moody, argumentative, or withdrawn. However, to determine if the behavior or attitude is cause for concern, it is important to note its frequency. A child who is occasionally flip or insolent is certainly not that unusual compared to a child who is fresh every time she talks to her parents. The more frequently the behavior is seen, the more it may deviate from normal.

Does the Behavior Interfere with the Teenager's Ability to Function in the Environment? All of us become depressed at times, but if this feeling or attitude prevents us from going to work or completing necessary duties around the house, then it should be a concern. If it does not significantly interfere with our daily functioning, however, then concern about this attitude and behavior can be somewhat minimized. Similarly, most children share an aversion to homework and some also to class work, but if this attitude or behavior results in failing grades or the necessity to attend summer school, then it may be considered not typical and should be a concern. If it does not restrict or prevent the teen from functioning like an average child, however, then parents need have less concern.

Does the Behavior Interfere with Others? Most siblings occasionally fight with one another, but if this type of behavior on the part of one child provokes a fearful or negative reaction on the part of the sibling, it may not be considered normal. A teenager who always fights with a younger sibling can disrupt the household from the time he comes home from school until the time he goes to bed. Conduct that significantly interferes with the routines, behaviors, and activities of other members of the household may deviate from the norm and be of concern.

3

Consider Individual Differences. Children have different personalities. One child may be sensitive, another talkative, a third shy, and so forth. In determining whether behavior is normal, you have to consider not only the teenager's peer group but also the individual child. For example, a teenager who has never been very talkative and who tends to bottle up her emotions may display this behavior at a higher degree when she reaches adolescence. A stubborn, strong-willed child may show more rebellion during adolescence than one who is compliant and passive.

In general, in trying to determine whether a behavior is normal or should be of concern, you can ask the following questions. How different is the behavior or attitude when compared with other children in her age group or her normal personality? How frequently does it occur? Does it interfere with others or with your child's ability to cope with her environment or to get along with people (not only her parents, but teachers, coaches, friends, neighbors, and others whom she deals with on a daily basis)?

4

2

THE ADOLESCENT'S PERCEPTION OF THE ENVIRONMENT

There is a quote in my office that says, "Until you have put yourself into the child's shoes and adjusted your approach to his understanding, you are not communicating at all. You are only talking to yourself." Probably the best way to understand the teenager's perception of the environment is to try to remember back to your own adolescence and recall some of the feelings, hopes, and ideas that you had. Many parents tend to forget about this period in their life when dealing with their own teenager. The following exaggerated example may help you to see the environment through the teenager's eyes.

Imagine that you are one of the brightest young people in the world. You know just about everything there is to know and your level of intelligence is equal to or perhaps just a little bit below that of Albert Einstein. Combined with this extremely high intellectual level, you have a tremendous amount of information about the world, life in general, what is important, and what is not important. Your vast intellect makes you aware of everything you should know and allows you to deal with most problem situations in a very effective manner.

Now imagine that you are employed by two mentally handicapped older persons with extremely limited knowledge of the world. Nevertheless, these two people are always telling you what you may or may not do. They also instruct you on how to do certain things and on what is important and unimportant. They ask you to perform tasks that do not make any sense, and usually you cannot see any logic behind their demands or requests. They talk about things that are unimportant or unrelated to your job or present situation. They continue to do so even after you have tried many times to make them realize that they do not know what they are talking about or that they do not understand a particular situation or that what they say has nothing to do with what is actually happening. They persist in harassing you with instructions, requests, demands, and irrelevant information that do not apply to what you are doing. In this situation, how would you feel?

For one thing, you would probably be angry much of the time because here are two people, intellectually your inferior, telling you what to do. If they told you to do something, you would probably do the opposite or do what you thought you needed to do rather than follow their request. You would also stay away from them as much as possible and spend more time with friends who understood things on your high level of comprehension. You would also probably forget to do some of the unimportant items they requested and instead become involved in activities you deemed important.

In the above example, you have probably been able to identify the teenager as the one with the high intellect and the parents as the intellectually inferior employers. The teen's peers usually are the only people considered to have intelligence approaching his own.

Adolescence used to occur around thirteen, fourteen, or fifteen years of age. However, today typical teenager behaviors and attitudes begin to emerge at ten and eleven years of age and sometimes even a little earlier.

To help you better understand this unsettled period, Keys 3 and 4 will discuss some of the changes that I see both in parents of adolescents and in the teenagers themselves that are not usually written about in books dealing with this stage of a child's life.

3

~~~~~~

PARENTAL CHANGES

While numerous changes are occurring in the adolescent, some corresponding changes are also occurring in the parents that may affect their ability to deal with their teenagers—for example, marital problems, depression, midlife crisis, financial difficulties, identity crisis, "empty nest" anxieties, difficulties in allowing their children to become adults, and other "real-life" problems. However, there are some other changes that occur that are not normally discussed or written about. Some examples follow.

Your Intelligence Decreases. I think it was Mark Twain who said something similar to, "When I was sixteen, my parents were very stupid. When I was twenty, it was amazing how much information and knowledge they had obtained in those four short years." Although there is no scientific evidence to back this theory, it seems as if the energy that is required for the child to develop physically during adolescence seems to be drained directly from the parent's brain. The end result is that we lose IQ points and become less intelligent than when the child was nine or ten years old. Because of this loss in intelligence, our logic and reasoning become faulty. We approach life and the world from a very limited capacity, and our ability to adequately provide information and direction is significantly reduced. In other words, we get dumber and do not know what we are talking about.

Physical Changes Occur. When your child enters adolescence, the person you see in your mirror seems to be the same as always. However, some changes have occurred that are imperceptible to you but very apparent to your teenager. Unfortunately, it is not known exactly what these specific changes are. It may be your dress, way of talking, physical appearance, actions, or hairstyle, but something has definitely changed for the worse. The youngster who in the past always wanted to be with you, now in adolescence does not want to be seen in your presence. It seems as if you have, for some unknown reason, become a total embarrassment to your child. Because of this unusual change in your physical appearance, attitude, or speech, your teenager may stop bringing his friends to the house because you embarrass him. If he or she does invite someone, they are more likely to spend the entire time locked in the teen's room to minimize any interaction with the parent. If you take the child to a basketball game or a movie, you may have to drop her off a block or two before the gym or around the corner from the movie so that none of the other intelligent people (translation: her peers) will see her with you. Teenagers do not like to be seen in public with their parents and when walking in a mall, they may proceed ten feet in front of or behind you. Although they used to like to go out to eat with you and to engage in other family activities, they now tend to avoid situations where people might think you are their parents. This even occurs in familiar settings such as relatives' or friends' houses. For example, every Sunday when you visited your parents you used to bring all the children; now the adolescent does not want any part of family gatherings.

Senility or Amnesia Develops. Either you slept through your own adolescence or you have total amnesia about this period in your life. You have no recall of what it is like to be a teenager and you do not understand what he or she is going through. Since you lack any idea of what it is like to be thirteen years old, there is no way you can relate to the teen's experiences, problems, needs, or desires.

This forgetfulness or amnesia centers around other things as well. Your cooking is one of the problems. You apparently have forgotten how to prepare meals, because almost everything you cook, your teenager does not want to eat. You could prepare a delicious seven-course meal, only to have your teen turn up his nose and eat a couple of cans of baked beans instead. You have also forgotten how to shop at the grocery store and never have anything good to eat in the house. Although you may have just spent $200 at the supermarket and have the refrigerator and cabinets stocked with food and snacks, the usual teen complaint is, "There's nothing to eat in this house." Perhaps part of not eating what you cook is the fact that they would have to sit at the dinner table with the family and, for some teenagers, this practice also becomes fairly unacceptable at this time. However, if you fix a dinner plate and leave it on the stove or put it in the refrigerator, you'll find it usually disappears later on. If your child would rather eat peanut butter and jelly sandwiches, Vienna sausage, or popcorn than the juicy T-bone steak you have prepared, I suggest you buy a supply of these foods for him and go enjoy your own dinner!

Parents of teenagers also become forgetful and tend to tell youngsters the same things over and over again. After hearing lecture number thirty-five several times in a week, they know it by heart and, in fact, can repeat most all of our lectures word for word. To help with your forgetfulness, it might be good if you could mark on the calendar the lecture and the time it was given to the child.

Regression Occurs. When your child was younger, it appears that you understood his situations, feelings, and needs. However, now that your child has reached adolescence, something has caused you to regress back in time to the "olden days," when you were young. You have become old-fashioned and are not "with it" anymore, and this interferes with your ability to understand your teenager. You constantly reminisce about the days when you were young. You listen to old-style music and do not know what the latest teen dress code is, how most people really act, or what other parents allow their children to do. You do not even know the names of the current rock groups. Be especially sure not to buy clothes for your child, because you have no earthly idea about what everybody is wearing. Even some other intellectually limited adults (your daughter's friends' parents) know more about what is happening than you do.

Your Ability to Communicate Decreases. When you talk to your teenagers, they look at you as if you are crazy and/or as if they do not understand anything you are saying. When you ask them to do something, it appears as if they do not hear you, or else they do just the opposite of what you have suggested or requested. Is it possible you have lost the ability to communicate effectively? When you talk to them, they either look at the ceiling or the floor, think about what they are going to do later in the day, or hum their favorite song, because nothing you say makes sense to them. Many of your conversations with them elicit just a blank stare. Either you have forgotten how to communicate or you are speaking a foreign language.

You Become Irritating. Sometimes your mere presence around the adolescent irritates him. Please do not ask even a simple question like "How was your day?" because that would tend to aggravate him and provoke a flippant response or even a dark look. Sometimes anything you do will annoy him.

Your Influence Decreases. During this adolescent period, what you say means very little to your child, and con-

11

sequently you have less influence over her behavior. Other people's opinions and values, especially those of her peers, become much more important than yours. In elementary school, the parents have a tremendous amount of influence over their child's behavior; no other person, thing, or event has as much impact on the child. In middle school, the parents' influence somewhat decreases but still has an impact on the child and is somewhat equal to the influence of peers and other factors. In high school, parental influence dramatically decreases and peer influence dramatically increases.

4

ADOLESCENT CHANGES

J ust as you experience many changes when your child hits this age range, teenagers also experience a number of changes.

Their Intelligence Increases. As discussed in Key 3, adolescent children suddenly become very smart and know almost everything there is to know. They are familiar with all subjects and know all the correct answers. I saw a sign one time that read, "Teenagers, tired of being hassled by your stupid and old-fashioned parents? Move out, get a job, and pay your own bills while you still know everything!"

Friends Become More Knowledgeable. Their friends' intelligence also markedly increases. Neighborhood children whom you have known for many years suddenly experience a dramatic surge in intellectual potential and become authorities in a variety of fields. If a friend says something, it is a fact and has to be true. It seems that when the mentally handicapped person [parent] says something, it does not mean much, but that when the advice comes from one of his peers, it must be true.

Communication Decreases. The young child who used to speak to you quite a bit and tell you everything that happened, now as a teenager has very little to say. She does not communicate often or at great length. In fact, responses

13

to your questions usually involve minimal verbal output and may consist of only one or two words. The child who used to share her feelings, attitudes, and opinions with you no longer seems to want to confide in you. But then, if the situation were reversed, you probably would not waste your time talking to stupid grownups who did not understand much about the world either.

Their Room Gains Importance. Teenagers tend to spend a great deal of time in their room. One probable reason is to escape nagging adults who do not understand anything that is happening with them. If they have a TV or phone in their room, you will only see them on the way to the bathroom or the refrigerator.

They also spend a great deal of time in their room because they sleep a lot. It appears that adolescents need a great deal of sleep. Getting up before noon on weekends is something you did when you were a kid.

Another change is the increased need for privacy. Like most adults, the teenager needs privacy—in his room, in visits with his friends, or in talking on the phone. Parents should respect the adolescent's right to privacy.

They Acquire Stocks. It seems as if teenagers believe they have inherited stock in the telephone company, specific radio stations, and/or CD companies. Therefore, they have to constantly talk on the phone or listen to the radio or CD player to make their stock more valuable. The parents' phone is always ringing because other teenagers also feel they have stock in the phone company. The more they use the phone, the higher the stock will go. Another adolescent belief is that the louder they play the radio or CD player, the more valuable their stock grows. Some teenagers must also think they have stock in the electric company because they never turn off electrical appliances or lights.

Anger Is Present. This age group often seems angry or resentful. Because of this anger, they frequently mumble and talk under their breath. If you ask them to do something, such as taking out the garbage, even as they perform the chore, they mutter under their breath, make faces, and shake their heads because these stupid adults interrupt their more important activities.

Peer Influence Increases. Peer groups are very important for teenagers. Because of adolescent desire to spend as much time as possible with individuals *similar* to them in intellectual ability, they tend to withdraw from family activities they used to enjoy (Sunday dinner at Grandma's), get highly insulted or annoyed if asked to do something with you, and would rather be with their friends than with parents. They might consider coming with you if you also invite one of their friends.

Moodiness Is Common. At this time, your child may be moody, get upset easily, and become quickly frustrated. These emotions are typical of this age. Mood swings often subside readily, although they may occur frequently.

A Dress Code Develops. Because of an unwritten adolescent dress code, teenagers want to dress like everybody else in their peer group, so that they appear to be in uniform. If a certain style or brand name of jeans or shoes is on the rapidly shifting dress-code list (much to the dismay of parents, who have to foot the bills), they must wear this and nothing else or they will be out of uniform.

Academic Interests Decline. Grades may decline. Disinterest in school may grow. When a child is between seven and ten years of age, he has a ten-pound bag and must put five pounds of activities and interests in it. At adolescence,

15

he still has the same ten-pound bag but now has to put twenty pounds of activities and interests in it. Football games, the opposite sex, talking on the phone, and parties crowd out schoolwork. Because of these additional interests and activities, grades may decline and the child may not do everything that he is supposed to do regarding his schoolwork.

Work Becomes a Four-Letter Word. Many parents describe their teenager as "lazy," but they don't mean the child is inactive. Teenagers just avoid work. They stay busy with their interests and activities, but ask them to do a job around the house or help with something that looks like work, and they disappear, find a hundred other things to do, or say, "I have tons of homework." Their primary job is to be an adolescent, and this demands the least amount of work possible. Their job involves having fun, talking on the phone, going places with their friends, listening to the CD player, and so on. Work is avoided because it interferes with their job.

These behaviors and attitudes are some of the typical ones found in the teenager. If your child shows some of these characteristics, she may be a typical adolescent and this should not arouse a great deal of concern. What should be of concern is how to deal with your child during this period. Much of this book helps parents deal effectively with typical teenage behaviors, as well as with problems that occur during this developmental stage.

5

WHAT HAVE I DONE
TO CAUSE
THIS BEHAVIOR?

Very frequently I hear parents say:

- My daughter is so moody and has such a negative attitude. What am I doing wrong?
- My son has more ability than my daughter, but he's failing two subjects and she's on the honor roll.
- I've treated all of my children the same. Why is he giving us trouble and not the others?
- My older daughter confides in me, and I always know how she is feeling and what is going on with her. However, my other daughter very seldom expresses any feelings and tends to keep to herself a lot.

The usual discussion that follows comments similar to the above centers around the parent's question "What have I done to cause this?" As indicated in the previous Key, certain behaviors emerge during adolescence that have very little to do with the parents' reaction to, or interaction with, their children. Some behaviors are a result of the youngsters' personalities and may already show certain characteristics.

While the environment certainly does influence, change, and mold behaviors, some mental health professionals unfortunately attribute to it *all* of the reasons that a child is having problems. In other words, they see the parents as the sole cause of the child's problems. Although the way we interact and deal with our children greatly affects their attitude and behavior, it is not true that parents are always responsible for all the problems seen in a child. Some children are capable of disrupting families, as much as families can interfere with healthy development in children. That is, a hyperactive child can certainly disrupt a family's ability to function, just as an alcoholic father can have a very negative effect on his family.

While the environment and the way we deal with our children certainly can shape personalities and develop behaviors, some children's personalities can be seen at a very young age. The parents of a stubborn and strong-willed child often relate that these characteristics were present during early childhood. At eighteen months this type of child often wanted to dress and bathe herself, and had a definite preference for what she wanted to wear or eat. Another child in the same family may have been more dependent and passive and would have let the parent dress him until he was eighteen if the parent wanted to.

All children do not feel, think, and act in the same ways. Although parents usually are able to recognize and acknowledge the *different* personality characteristics in their children, they will often use the *same* methods in trying to manage, discipline, or teach their children. What may work for one child will not necessarily work for another. You and I do not treat all adults the same way. For example, you might say to one of your friends, "Boy, did you get fat," and he will laugh and joke about it. However, if you tell another person this, you may hurt his feelings. Therefore, depending on individual personalities, you would treat people differently. The same holds true when dealing with children.

The behavior that we see in our children is a result of the interaction between their personality and the environment (the family situation, how they are treated). Therefore, if your child becomes president of the United States, you cannot take all the credit. On the other hand, if he causes trouble in school or shows other inappropriate behaviors, you cannot assume all the blame. The child's behavior is the combined result of his personality (the characteristics with which he was born) and the way he is managed or dealt with (the environment).

If the techniques you are using work with some of your children but not with others, the methods themselves are not wrong or inappropriate. They are just not the right techniques for that particular child. If they were bad, they would not work for any of the children. The technique you use to deal with a certain behavior in your daughter may be good and work beautifully with her, but it does not work with your son, who has a different personality. Place your son in another environment (deal with him differently), and you might see entirely different reactions and behaviors. The more techniques you have to deal with your child's behavior, the greater the chance that you will be successful.

When dealing with teenagers, parents should keep in mind that children are individuals. Therefore, individual methods must be used to increase the probability of success. A child's behavior is a result of the interaction between his personality and the environment. Although the environment—that is, the way you deal with your children—is not always the entire reason a child behaves in a certain way, you can produce changes in behavior by modifying the environment and varying the techniques or methods you are using.

19

6

▲▲

YOUR CHILD IS BECOMING A YOUNG ADULT

While many of the adolescent changes that were described in the preceding Key irritate parents and cause some problems within the family unit, they can be viewed as part of normal adolescent development. The stubbornness, independence, and movement away from parental values usually reflects healthy growth and the teenager's movement toward adulthood. Some of the typical behaviors seen at this time are attempts by the teenager to deal with monumental developmental tasks. A few examples will help clarify the picture.

There is a developmental need to separate from the family that teenagers found so comfortable in the middle years of their childhood. Adolescents are on a lonely road between the family of their childhood and their final destinations in adulthood. This is not a road they can escape. To accomplish this task, they often latch on to idealized peer values and devalue the opinions, judgments, and actions of their parents and family. They spend much time in their rooms alone, not because of contempt for their parents, but in search of themselves. In this lonely effort, alienated, they may also look elsewhere for acceptance and love, often in the wrong places.

Throughout the teenage years there is the developmental process of *identity formation*—that is, the development of a unique identity, a person with values, self-definitions, aspirations, and directions. This identity is formed largely through experimentation with, and differentiation from, parental values. It is this phenomenon that accounts for much of the debate of adolescence, the teenager's contrariness—his needs to behave, dress, and think differently from his parents. Parents need to understand this and not brand it as thoughtless arrogance alone.

A different level of thinking develops during this period of growth. Teenagers develop the ability to think on an abstract level as they are sorting out and consolidating their identities. They think about the profound questions of who they are, what is important, what will be the meaning of their lives, what do they believe in. They judge the world around them, partly according to those questions that they ask themselves. This is healthy. They can become radically idealistic, especially in contrast to the values and lifestyles of their parents, which results from inevitable pragmatism and compromise.

Changing Your Technique of Dealing with Your Child. Many changes are occurring in the adolescent and, as parents, we also make corresponding changes to effectively relate to, deal with, and interact with our child. Generally, in dealing with your teenager, you should try to use techniques that will not produce further rebellion, opposition, anger, and defiance, because there already is enough of this type of behavior and attitude present.

Probably the most important adjustment that parents must make is to realize they are no longer dealing with a child, but with a *young adult*. Many techniques that work with the younger child will not work with the adolescent or will create more problems than they solve. In a sense, par-

21

ents can control the younger child, but this type of approach does not work well with an adolescent.

A lot of confusion occurs during this time on the part of both parent and child. The teenager who asks to be treated like an adult may still be acting like a child. At the same time, the parent who tells the adolescent to act more mature and grown-up is still treating the youngster like a child. With young children we have a tendency to nag, remind, or force them to do certain things. By adolescence this process must change, and we must move into an adult method of dealing with the teenager's behavior.

There are several concepts and techniques to keep in mind when making the transition from dealing with a child to dealing with a young adult.

Avoid Power Struggles. Any time you get into a power struggle or control battle with an adolescent, you automatically lose. You want to avoid either forcing children to do certain things or getting into power struggles with them. If they refuse to cooperate, set some rules and consequences that you can enforce and control.

Some parents fight battles with their children and feel that they must always win the conflict—that is, they must control the child and make him do exactly what he is told or is supposed to do. These parents are continually fighting battles, but never win the war. The major part of this approach involves power struggles with the adolescent (clean your room, cut the grass, get off the phone).

Sometimes it is better to focus on winning the war and forget about winning individual battles. In other words, shift to a different type of control. It may be better to have the adolescent *experience the consequences* of not doing what was requested of her rather than *make* her do what is asked. Hopefully, after this occurs a few times, you may be able to get more cooperation from her. An example would be that of a teenager whose allowance is based on cutting the grass. She is told on Monday that the grass has to be cut by 7:00 P.M. Friday in order for her to receive her allowance. Rather than constantly reminding her all week about the grass, the parent should tell her once and just let it go. It may be more important for her to forfeit her allowance because of not cutting the grass on time than for the parent to make her cut the grass. By approaching the child in this fashion, you can avoid power struggles, nagging, and yelling, and use a more passive or laid-back control.

In a sense, we should deal with the adolescent in a fashion similar to the way we deal with our friends or other adults. For example, let us suppose that you are working for me and I tell you "I want you to complete all the paperwork on your desk and I don't want you leaving the office this afternoon until you finish everything." You reply, "I'm not going to do the paperwork. You can't make me. I don't see why I have to do it and I'm not going to!" Now, since we are both adults, I would not nag you, keep reminding you, give you a lecture on responsibility, or physically force you to do it. I would simply say, "If you do the work and have it completed today, you're still working for me; if not, you're fired." So, in a sense, what I am saying is that I would like you to do this work, but I really don't care what you do. Do whatever you want to. But I'm going to be sure that one thing will happen if you comply with my request (you will keep your job) and something entirely different will result if you do not follow my instructions (you will be fired). Key 24 and Key 26 provide more detailed information regarding the avoidance of power struggles and this type of management technique.

Improve Communication. Because adolescents are not usually willing to talk much to parents, we do not have a lot of communication with them. Unfortunately, much of our conversation with the adolescent is concerned with getting a point across, teaching him something, correcting him, or with some other subject that tends to emphasize the negative behaviors or faults of the child. Therefore, the majority of our verbal interaction with adolescents has a negative implication or is seen by them as a lecture. We should try to improve communication by discussing more positive behaviors and things that interest them (their hobbies, sports, dancing, music, clothing). We should also try to establish times during the day that we can converse with them with the sole purpose of having a positive interaction with them.

Because the number of consequences (rewards, punishments) available to parents decreases dramatically when the child becomes an adolescent, it is important to become aware of your child's feelings, needs, wants, likes, and dislikes. This can be accomplished through an increase in communication. See Keys 18, 19, and 20 for additional suggestions in this area.

Try to Compromise. This technique involves both of the concepts just mentioned: *improving communication* and *avoiding power struggles*. If we can get the child to express more of his likes, dislikes, and feelings, we will have more opportunities to compromise and to avoid power struggles and battles. An example that I frequently use with adolescents follows: Let's say that I ask you to help me wash the kitchen windows. You really do not want to, but you need a ride to the shopping center. Rather than your telling me, "No, I don't want to do this work," or my forcing you to do it ("Whether you like it or not, you must do it!"), it would be better for both of us to agree on a compromise. You will help me with the windows and I'll take you to the mall.

Rather than having a winner and a loser, the compromise sets up a situation where both people win. Set up situations where both child and parent can win. If the adolescent wants to stay out later or use the car more frequently, find areas that you would like to have him improve and use those as a method of compromise. For example: "You can use the car an additional night if you study more." Use compromises to obtain the behaviors you desire.

With the compromise you are basically saying, "I know what you want and you know what I want. If you cooperate with me, I'll be sure to cooperate with you. If you do not cooperate with me, don't expect me to cooperate with you." In a sense, you are treating the adolescent the way you would treat another adult or friend.

Avoid the Buildup of Anger. Remember our earlier example of a rebellious and angry "employee" (adolescent) whose mentally handicapped "employer" (parents) are constantly instructing him in what to do, even though they themselves know very little about the meaning of life? Part of the picture is true, in that many teens often feel angry with parents and authority. A certain amount of anger, resistance, and rebellion is typical of this age group. Therefore, you should try to prevent the buildup of additional anger by reducing the amount of criticism, negative attention, and correction you give your teen and by avoiding as much confrontation as possible. See Key 22 for more information.

Recognize Normal Adolescent Behavior. The child is becoming a young adult, and his behaviors, attitudes, and opinions are changing. It is time that you become familiar with normal adolescent behaviors because you are starting to lose your child and gain a young adult. Many times I hear parents say, "My child has changed. I wish I had the old one back." Upon further questioning, the new model is described as less communicative, sometimes fresh, somewhat uncooperative, and moody; but basically what the parents are

25

describing are typical adolescent behaviors. If you view some of these normal behaviors as problems and try to "bring back" the behavior of the young child, you may increase the distance between you and the teenager and more problems may develop than are solved.

A large part of dealing with this new person that lives in your house is to try to cope with these normal changes in a fashion that will minimize additional conflict, emotional distance between the parents and teenagers, decreases in communication, or withdrawal from the family. The information in the following Keys will help you accomplish this.

7

DEALING WITH DAILY BEHAVIORS

P arents express many specific concerns about the adolescent's attitudes and behaviors. However, before addressing some of the specific topics in later Keys, here is some general information on effective techniques of behavior management that should help you deal with your child on a daily basis. How do you get the child to cooperate more around the house? What can you do to get him to clean his room or to have him come in on time? How do you improve her flippant attitude or get her to stop aggravating her sister?

Some of the techniques presented here are guaranteed to make your day run smoother and reduce some conflict in your home. I suggest you read this Key before proceeding with the rest of the book because many of the Keys that follow are based on the techniques presented here.

In general, you will first want to analyze the behavior you are trying to deal with. Then spell out the rule or expectation *and* the consequence at the same time, *before* the rule is broken. Say what you mean and mean what you say. Follow through with what you say and be consistent.

Analyze the Behavior. In discussing the adolescent's behavior, many parents remark: "He does not want to be part of the family," "My daughter is depressed and unhappy," "She's not motivated in school," "His problem is he's always angry," "My son is constantly irritating everybody," "She is immature." My first response is to ask the parent, "Can you give me an example of what you mean when you say he does not want to be part of the family?" "What behavior is the child showing that makes you think he is angry?" "What is he doing to irritate everybody?" "What is your child doing that makes you think she is immature?" In other words, I ask the parents to look at the behavior in more specific terms rather than in general terms. What I mean when I say, "My daughter is depressed," might be that she has lost interest in things that were important to her. What you mean when you say, "My daughter is depressed," might be that she stays in her room all the time and cries easily. Lack of motivation in school could mean a variety of things: the child is capable of A's and B's, but is getting only C's; she is not studying for tests; she does not complete homework; or she daydreams in class.

Be Specific. Before any behavior can be dealt with or changed, it first must be specified or stated in detail. Although it might not be possible to *make* your son become more a "part of the family," you may be able to get him to spend more time out of his room and become more involved in family interaction. If you say your teen is angry, what exactly is he doing? Is he continually muttering under his breath, making faces when you try to tell him something, slamming doors, or generally getting very upset and volatile over minor difficulties? What is the immaturity you worry about in your daughter? Is she fifteen years old and does she still need your help in getting dressed for school?

Many parents find it somewhat difficult to look at specific behaviors, because it is normal to talk about our children in very general terms. However, the first step in changing any behavior is to be specific. Try to avoid vague, general terms, and identify the exact behavior or behaviors that are of concern and what you would like to change.

Look at the Behavior Sequence. Once the behavior has been described in detail, you can then analyze the entire behavior sequence. For example, let's take the child who will never take no for an answer. How did he get this way?

Parent: My child will never accept no for an answer.

Psychologist: What do you mean by that? Can you give me an example?

Parent: I just can't tell him no. If everything is going his way and he is getting to do whatever he wants and is not told no, everything is fine. However, when we tell him he cannot do what he wants, he gets upset and argues and cannot accept what we have told him. He used our car all last week; then last night when he asked to use the car again, we refused and he became very upset and started arguing.

Psychologist: What did he say to you?

Parent: He was really shouting and told us how mean we were and how all his friends' parents let them use the car whenever they wanted to. He also mentioned that we used to let his brother have the car whenever he wanted and that we were putting too many restrictions on him. We were not being fair and did not understand his situation.

Psychologist: What did you do?

Parent: We told him that we need to use the car and that he just could not have it whenever he wanted. A car is expensive to operate and he would have to try to use it less often and get rides with his friends. He can have it to go specific places, not just to joyride all around the city. After many attempts to try to reason calmly with him and explain why we said no, my husband and I became upset with his attitude and unwillingness to see our position.

Psychologist: What happened next?

29

Parent: Because he had an answer for everything we told him, pretty soon we started arguing back at him. After a while, we became totally exasperated and tired of the verbal battle, so we gave him the keys to the car and told him to leave in order for us all to calm down.

In the above example, if the child listened to his parents he would not use the car. However, by aggravating, not taking "no" for an answer, he was able to use the car. The reason this behavior occurs—and continues—is because it works!

Let's take another example, the child who does not cooperate without an argument or fuss and always has something to say if you ask her to do something.

Parent: Every time I ask my child to do something she complains, "I'm not a slave. Why do I have to do this? My brother doesn't have to. You're always making me do things." She has just a few jobs to do around the house, but each time we ask her, she'll either put off the chore and not do it or give us a hard time.
Psychologist: Give me an example of what you mean.
Parent: The other night I asked her to put out the garbage. She started mumbling and complaining and making faces, then grabbed the garbage can and dragged it out to the curb, banging it every inch of the way. You would think I had asked her to paint the house or resod the lawn.
Psychologist: But she did put out the garbage?
Parent: Yes, but the whole time she was complaining and acting as if she did not want to do what she was asked.
Psychologist: What did you do next?
Parent: I tried to ignore most of what she said but she was starting to irritate me, so I began explaining everything that her father and I did for her. I asked how she would like it if every time she asked us to do something

we made a scene or complained. I told her that she had only a few chores to do and that I did not feel as if it were a burden for her to do a few simple things for me when I did so much for her. She continued mumbling and I continued yelling, and she eventually stalked off to her room.

In situations like the above, what I have asked the parents to do is to analyze the behavior. They should not only look at the **behavior**—the unwillingness to take no for an answer (example 1) or the mumbling and complaining (example 2)—but also look at what comes before the behavior (**antecedents**) and what comes after it (the **consequence**). In any behavior sequence there are three parts:

ANTECEDENTS, BEHAVIOR, AND CONSEQUENCE: A→B→C

A ——————▶ B ——————▶ C		
Antecedents	**Behavior**	**Consequence**
Asks to use the car. Told, "No."	Will not accept. Argues.	Gets to use the car.
Told to do a chore	Mumbles. Complains.	Parent gets upset.

In looking at the entire behavior sequence, we have taken the first step in dealing with the behavior. We have not only looked at the specific behavior, but have also seen what comes before the action and what comes after it. We have to look at the entire sequence before attempting to change it.

In analyzing a behavior, it is also important to see how often it occurs—that is, how many times a day, hour, or week. Does it occur ten times a day, once a week, or three times an hour? There are a couple of reasons for looking at how frequently a behavior occurs. I have had many parents tell me, "Once I started looking at the behavior closely and keeping a record of how frequently it occurred, I realized

31

that it was not as bad as I thought it was. I thought he and his brother were fighting continuously but the fights only occurred a couple of times a day." Another reason for looking at frequency of behavior is that the child usually does not wake up one morning behaving a certain way. The behavior develops gradually over a period of weeks, months, or years. Therefore, in changing the behavior, a similar process will occur. A gradual improvement over time will take place.

Usually, when parents look at the child's actions in general terms (e.g., anger, immaturity, uncooperativeness), they cannot see the small changes that occur. For example, parents may tell me, "Our child never talks to us. He never communicates anything and we don't know what is going on in his life." I might then try some interventions and give the parents suggestions to improve the communication. After a few weeks, if the parents looked only at the overall behavior, they might still feel the child was uncommunicative and not as talkative as he used to be when he was younger. However, if they had observed the child's behavior more closely in order to see how frequently he was communicating, they might have seen an improvement. They might have realized that before the treatment plan was started, the child spoke to them only a couple of times or only when he needed something. However, after a few weeks of trying some interventions, the child was now communicating five to seven times a day and was volunteering information about school, friends, and activities. Looking at the overall behavior and comparing it to when the child was younger, it may still seem as if he is not talking very much. However, if we look at the frequency of the behavior knowing that behavior changes gradually, we can see a considerable improvement from when the treatment plan was started. We have to look for small improvements and movements toward a goal and not for a dramatic change overnight.

In analyzing behavior in this way, we look at the important factors in behavior change—the consequences. The reason most of us do what we do is that we know the consequences of our behavior. If the consequences of behavior were always the same, and, for example, you were paid whether you went to work or stayed home, you would be foolish to go to work. The same holds true for adolescents. The teenagers in the two examples behaved the way they did because they already knew the consequences of their behavior. They got what they wanted.

The following may be somewhat similar to what goes on unconsciously, or sometimes consciously, with your child.

Psychologist: Your mother tells me that you never do anything the first time you are told. She has to tell you over and over again and get upset and yell before you do anything, such as cleaning your room.

Adolescent: My mother is always talking and telling me to do stuff. She gives me a hundred lectures a day and asks me to do a lot of stupid things, like cleaning my room. I usually put off doing what she says because the first thirty times she tells me, she uses a normal tone of voice and is pretty calm, so I don't think she really means it.

Psychologist: Then what happens?

Adolescent: Around the thirty-first time, her voice starts getting a little bit louder. She's getting upset now, and around the thirty-second or thirty-third time, she starts hollering and saying in a very angry voice, "I really mean it. You'd better clean your room!" Somewhere around the thirty-fourth and thirty-fifth time she says it, the vein in her neck starts sticking out, her face turns red, and she's really screaming now.

Psychologist: What do you do then?

Adolescent: Well, finally I know she means business, because the hair on the back of her neck is standing up. So I go clean the room or do whatever else she wants me to do.

Psychologist: It sounds as if you wait for the right signal or cue that tells you a consequence is coming or something is really going to happen. When you know she means business, that's when you do what your mother requests.

Adolescent: That's right.

There are many other examples that could be used, but the point is that people often behave as they do because of the consequences of their behavior—what they get out of it or what happens to them as a result of it. Many behaviors in the adolescent are present because of the consequences. Whenever people relate to or interact with one another, parents and adolescents included, they teach each other certain behaviors based primarily on consequences. When we interact with our children, we are teaching them behaviors and they are teaching us to respond to them in certain ways. We may teach children how to be dependent, fresh, or immature, or how not to take no for an answer, not to listen, or the like. At the same time, they may teach us how to scold, nag, scream, get upset, criticize, or worry. It stands to reason that if we can teach children certain unacceptable behaviors, we can also teach them acceptable behaviors. This is true, but most of us go about it the wrong way, by focusing directly on the children and trying to change them. It is very difficult to change another's behavior without changing our own. It is much easier if parents change the way they relate to their teenagers, and, as a result, the youngsters change their behavior and the way they relate to the parents. I am *not* implying, as some mental health professionals do, that parents are the cause of *all* behavior difficulties in children. Children can cause problems in a family, as well as parents can cause problems in children. However, it is easier for adults to change their behavior than to try directly to change the teenager's behavior.

Much of the behavior seen in people is the result of consequences and a person's response to environmental conditions. Often, without a change in environment, it will be difficult to change the behavior. If the surroundings and reactions of others are modified, however, it will be easier to alter it. While it is much easier to modify a young child's environment than an adolescent's, your behavior and your response to the child are part of the environment and can be changed. By responding to children differently, you can change the influence of their behavior. Just as important as analyzing the child's behavior, parents need to look closely at what they themselves are doing and how they are responding to situations. If parents can change both their reactions and the types of consequences used to deal with the teenager, they in turn may modify their teenager's behavior.

8

BEING A CONSISTENT
PARENT

A very common behavior in adolescents is that they do not listen to their parents. When a parent talks to them, the message goes in one ear and out the other. One reason teenagers do not listen to parents is that adults often do not mean what they say or follow through on what they say. This simple concept is extremely important to keep in mind in any type of dealings with your teenager. Inconsistency on the part of the parent is often the basis for not listening and is one of the main reasons that techniques tried by parents do not work.

We do not listen to adults who say one thing and do something else, so we cannot expect our teenagers to listen to us if we behave in the same way.

There are many ways in which parents are inconsistent and thereby confuse children or teach them to be manipulative or not to listen. Some examples follow.

Empty Statements.
- Unless you come in right now, I'm going to break both your legs.
- If you don't straighten up in school, I am going to send you to boarding school.
- I'll kill you if you don't stop bothering me.
- If you and your brother don't stop fighting, I'm leaving home and never coming back.

I'm sure you could think of many other similar statements where parents say things they have no intention of
carrying out. The adult knows this, but, more importantly,
the child knows it too. Therefore, using threats like these
will not stop the behavior and the child will continue the
behavior you are trying to modify.

Overstatements.

• Go to your room. You are punished until you are 18 years old.

• You cannot talk on the phone for the entire school year.

• You are grounded for a month.

Overstatements like these are also a major source of
inconsistencies in families. Parents get angry and make a
promise or threat they can never keep. Or they say or do
something and then start feeling guilty. As the guilt
increases, they may try to do something to undo the comment or reduce the punishment if the child shows appropriate behavior. However, in both instances, the child interprets
the parents' behavior as saying, "Don't believe or listen to
what I say because I don't really mean it."

Turning "No" to "Yes" and "Yes" to "No." In this
situation, the parent says one thing and does something else.
Remember the example of the teenager who asks to use the
car and is told "No"? The youngster does not accept this
answer and starts to harass his parents. After a time the parents give in and let him use the car in order to end the argument and preserve their sanity. Here, the original "no" has
been changed to "yes." How many times have you promised
something like this: "I'll take you shopping Saturday. We can
also practice your driving this weekend. And I'll help you
work on your car this Sunday"? However, when the time
comes you say, "I'm a little too busy this weekend. We'll do it
next weekend."

The major point here is that a "no" has been changed to a "yes," or vice versa, that a positive statement has become negative. Not only are we teaching our children not to listen to us when we respond in this fashion, but we are also showing them how to manipulate us. In other words, we are saying, "If I tell you something that you do not like, do this [complain, get me upset, argue] and I'll change my mind." This type of inconsistency should also be avoided.

Not Checking Up on the Behavior. You can also show inconsistency by telling your child to do something and not checking to see that it has been done. You tell your son that he cannot leave the house until he cleans his room. He goes in his room while you are busy somewhere else in the house. In a few minutes he comes out and says, "I'm leaving." You ask, "Did you clean your room?" and he responds positively and leaves. Half an hour later you happen to pass his room and notice that he has not picked up a thing.

The necessity to check on behavior and performance is not important in the case of some adolescents, but for others you have to follow up and see if the child has done what he was asked to do or what he was supposed to do. Some children will try to get away with as much as possible if you let them. This form of inconsistency on the part of the parent tends to interfere with the development of responsibility and also teaches children to be manipulative.

Consistency from Both Parents. The examples used all pertain to the need for consistency from each parent. In other words, both parents need to be very predictable in dealing with their teenager. If one tells a child that he cannot use the car until the room is clean, the child should be able to bet his life that the only way he is going to be able to drive the car is to clean his room.

Consistency must come from both mother and father as a unit. Each parent must mean what he or she says when dealing with the child, but they must also support and back up one another. A child asks his mother, "Can I go to a concert tonight?" She says, "No." Then he asks his father the same question and gets a positive answer. Now it is almost time for the concert and the child starts getting dressed to go. His mother sees him and asks him what he is doing and where he is going and he responds by telling her that he is going to the concert and that his father said he could. The mother then confronts the father and an argument starts. In the meantime, the son finishes getting dressed and leaves for the concert.

Parents can create inconsistency by undermining each other and not presenting a unified approach to the child. By doing this, several things happen. First, the child learns to play one parent against the other and to manipulate them to get his way. Also, when one parent disciplines a child or makes a decision and the other contradicts the action, the first parent's authority is reduced and, consequently, the child views one parent as holding authority and may not listen to the other. In addition, this type of approach tends to identify one parent as the "bad guy" or the mean one and the other as the "good guy," the benevolent one. If you happen to be the bad guy, look out! This type of inconsistency also produces arguing and fighting between parents.

It is extremely important for parents and relatives (aunts, uncles, grandparents) who frequently deal with the teenager to be consistent as a unit. If you disagree with your partner or another person who has a significant part in disciplining your child, it is best to support the other person in front of your child. Later, when your child is not around, discuss the situation and, more importantly, resolve it. If the punishment is to be reduced, the person who established the consequence should be the one who modifies it.

Different Reactions to the Same Behavior. Depending on what mood we are in or how the day has gone, we often treat the same behavior in different ways. For example, one day a child may be insolent and we react to his impudence by giving him a lecture. The next day the same type of behavior occurs and we ignore it. The following day the behavior is seen again and we restrict the child from some type of privilege, and so forth. Rather than reacting differently, it might be better for you to set up a standard rule that whenever your teen acts up or talks back, he or she will lose some phone privileges or be grounded for a certain period. Setting up rules and consequences in this fashion will reduce this type of inconsistency and make the environment more structured and predictable. It is important to spell out the rule and the consequence at the same time (see Key 9 for further information).

Environmental Consistency. So far, the discussion of consistency has related to how adults interact with teenagers. But is the child able to predict the adult? This type of consistency, called *interpersonal consistency*, is probably the most important type and is essential for effective behavior management. In addition, consistency, structure, or routine in the environment sometimes reduces behavioral difficulties also. For example, a child who has a set time to get off the phone will usually cause less trouble for the parent than one who is allowed to talk for different time lengths each night. A child who has a particular time to come home will often give the parent less trouble than one who does not. In general, environmental consistency—that is, consistency of routines—should be established if you are having trouble with a particular behavior.

40

Consistency might seem like a minor concept but it is a major principle in behavior management. It serves as a foundation on which other techniques and methods are built. A good rule to keep in mind when interacting with your adolescent is: *Do not say anything you can't do or don't want to do, and do everything you say you are going to do.* You have to follow through in order to deal effectively with the child.

9

SETTING RULES/ EXPECTATIONS AND CONSEQUENCES

A dolescents are very much into the "fairness" concept; that is, they respect and respond to parents, teachers, and other authority figures whom they perceive as being fair. Teenagers are less responsive to parents who they feel do not understand them and treat them in an unfair or unjust way. One of the ways to avoid being perceived as unfair and instead to present yourself to the adolescent as a fair and just person is to establish the rules and the consequences for behavior at the same time.

Most parents have a hundred rules and regulations around the house. For example: "Come home at 11:00 P.M." "Cut the grass." "After you use the bathroom, be sure you leave it the way you found it." "All of your homework must be done before you talk on the phone." Parents are usually good in specifying what they want or in setting rules. They state the expectation beautifully, but, unfortunately, many wait until the rule is broken before deciding what the consequence will be. For example, if a child is told to be home by 11:00 and shows up at 11:30, the parent then decides what is going to happen—whether he will be grounded for a week or is not allowed out the next night or is restricted from using the phone. This method of announcing the consequence after the rule is broken is viewed as unfair by youngsters and should be avoided.

When we discipline or try to enforce rules and expectations in this fashion, several things happen.

First of all, in this situation, the child does not feel responsible for what has happened to him nor does he feel in control of the consequences of his behavior. As a result, he does not develop responsibility nor does he feel that he can influence what happens to him.

Also, if we wait until the adolescent breaks the rule to decide the punishment or consequence, the teen is likely to develop anger toward the parent because he feels that the parent is responsible for the bad thing (the consequence) that has happened to him. Since many adolescents already have some underlying anger, it is not helpful to do anything that will produce more resentment.

Rules and Consequences Should Be Stated at the Same Time. In setting rules, parents should avoid stating only the expectation. It is important to spell out both the rule and the consequence at the same time and *before* the rule is broken.

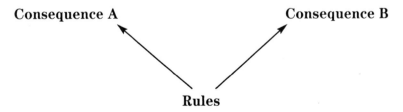

Consequence A   **Consequence B**

Rules

The above diagram indicates the way effective rules should be set. That is, you should tell the child, "Here is what I want you to do. This (Consequence A) will happen if you do it that way, and this (Consequence B) will happen if you do it the other way." By using this method, you allow the child to decide for himself what is going to happen to him.

By stating the rules and the consequences at the same time, you put the responsibility for what happens to the teenager squarely on his shoulders. In terms of discipline, you become passive and laid-back and do exactly what the child tells you to do. This approach should eliminate nagging or power struggles. The teenager is in control of the consequences of his behavior and determines whether good or bad things happen to him.

Consequences are the most important tool in changing behavior and the method just described is the most effective way to use them. You may not be able to employ this technique all of the time but should use it whenever possible.

Rules and Consequences Have to Be Specific. How many times has something like this happened to you? The teenager's room has been a mess for three weeks and it seems as if everything she owns is on the floor. You tell her, "Go to your room and pick up everything off the floor." About fifteen minutes later she comes out and you ask, "Did you do what I said?" Her response is "Yes." You go in the room to check and find that all the junk that was on the floor is now on the bed. You get upset, but what has happened is that she has taken you literally and fulfilled your expectation 100 percent: she has picked everything up off the floor.

Teenagers often do exactly what you tell them and usually have their own definitions of words. You should try to be as specific as possible when stating rules or behavioral expectations. If you say, "I want you to go to your room and clean it," you need to define what you mean by *clean*. "Put the dirty clothes in the hamper, the books on the shelf, and the trash and paper that are on the floor in the wastebasket. And don't put anything under your bed."

Parents may encounter problems in management if the expectations are stated in too general or cloudy terms—for example: "I want you to improve in school." or "Be nice to your sister." What do "improve" and "be nice" mean? They can mean different things to different people. To the teenager, improving in school might mean getting all D's instead of F's, and being nice to his sister might mean that he hits her only ten times a day instead of twenty-five. On the contrary, the parent defines improving in school as earning a C average and being nice to the sister as not hitting her at all. Therefore, if the expectations are not specific enough, when the parent and teenager get together to compare notes they come up with a difference of opinion. The child feels that he has fulfilled the expectation, but the parent does not. Therefore, a situation has been created where the teenager thinks he has been unfairly treated.

The same thing happens when parents state the consequences in too general or vague terms. "If you do that again, you're going to get it." "You'll be punished if you don't improve in school." What does "going to get it" or "punished" mean to the teenager? Probably not very much.

In stating expectations/rules and consequences, you must be very specific and spell out what you mean. Do not assume that the adolescent "knows." Both parent and teenager have to have the same idea of what is expected and what the consequences will be. If the child is not sure, he is apt to be confused, feel resentful, or think he has been treated unfairly.

45

10

TECHNIQUES TO SET RULES AND CONSEQUENCES

Expectations and consequences must be spelled out ahead of time in order for them to be most effective. Both the child and the parent must know exactly what behavior is expected and what consequences will follow.

There are three general ways that this can be accomplished.

Use Natural Consequences. Some behaviors carry with them natural consequences, and these consequences are often sufficient to produce change and a good way to start. A few examples follow.

- "I serve supper between 5:00 and 6:00 P.M. The kitchen closes at 6:00." The child who comes home at 6:30 is faced with the natural consequence of not eating or of preparing his own meal.

- "I only wash clothes that are placed in the hamper." The natural consequences of not putting clothes where they belong are that you cannot wear them, you wash them yourself, or you wear them dirty.

- "I am giving you your allowance on Friday. This is supposed to last until next Friday. I will not give you any more money until then." The natural consequences of going out

Friday night and spending your entire allowance is that you will not have any money for the remainder of the week.

- "Anyone who breaks something in the house will be responsible for paying for the repair." The natural consequence of slamming a door and breaking it is that the person who slammed it will have to come up with the money to pay for it.

The natural consequence that I frequently use in dealing with the teenager centers around cooperation in the home. In other words, the parent is telling the child, "If you cooperate with me, I'll cooperate with you. Everyone here has certain chores and responsibilities. If I have to pick up after you because you fail to do your job, I will have to use some of my free time to do what you were supposed to do. Therefore, I will not have time to do what you want."

Many teenagers feel that their parents are always on their back, asking them to do too many things. They complain, "I wish my parents would leave me alone and let me do what *I* want." Some teenagers feel as though they do ten things for their parents for every one thing the parents do for them. Frequently, natural consequences are used to deal with this situation. The parent might tell the child, "You don't want me to ask you to do things, and you want me to quit hassling you. Well, I'll be more than happy to do this, but, remember, if I don't ask you to do things for me, you can't ask me to do things for you." At first the child thinks this is a good deal. But after a while she realizes that she is getting the short end of the deal and that the parent does more for her than she realized.

Many approaches to teenage behavior stress natural or logical consequences as methods of dealing with it. However, two things must be kept in mind when using natural conse-quences.

First, the natural consequence has to be important to the child in order for it to be effective. For example, the nat-ural consequence of telling a teenager "I will not wash any of your clothes that are not put in the clothes hamper" will not work effectively for a child who does not care whether he wears clean or dirty outfits.

The other thing to consider before using this technique is if you want the natural consequence to occur. One morn-ing at 4:00 A.M. I got a call from a very upset mother. She told me that her thirteen-year-old son had left the house at seven o'clock the previous evening and was not yet home. When I asked what had happened, she told me that the boy and his father had had an argument about cleaning his room. When the child refused, the father responded angrily, "This is my house and as long as you live here you have to do what I want you to do, and I am telling you to clean your room!" After quite a bit of arguing, the father eventually warned, "If you don't like the rules in this house, you can leave," and the child left. The child experienced the natural consequence in this situation, but of course the parents did not want this to be the outcome.

In using this technique, parents must respond in a very matter-of-fact manner. You should try not to become upset, shout, or carry on. You have to be sure that the consequence is important to the child and you must consistently follow through with what is said.

Use Grandma's Rule. This is a principle that most par-ents can use frequently. It can be stated very simply as, "You do what I want you to do and then you can do what you want to do." Or, "You do what I want you to do and then I'll do what you want me to do." Similarly, your mother may have promised, "Eat your meat and potatoes, and then you can have your dessert." Natural consequences are things that are built into the environment, whereas this method of setting consequences can be ad-libbed and used on the spur of the moment. See Key 9 for specific guidelines.

Use Important Consequences. When either natural consequences or Grandma's Rule cannot be used, you should try to identify consequences that are important to the child and to set the rules of behavioral expectations according to these. The consequences can be positive, things that do not happen every day at your house (extra phone time, staying out late, or having a friend sleep over). They can also be negative (loss of privileges, grounding, restrictions). Any privilege, activity, or request that is important to the child can serve as a consequence of his behavior.

- The child who wants to stay out later on the weekend may earn this privilege through more involvement in schoolwork during the week.
- Extra phone time or having a friend sleep over may be earned by a child who makes an effort to get along better with his siblings.
- An allowance could be earned by doing chores.

Positive consequences like the above enable a child to obtain a privilege or have a request granted.

Another method of using important consequences would be to set up situations where the teenager is being restricted or is losing particular privileges by behaving in certain ways.

- The child who talks back to his parents may not get the new tennis shoes he wanted.

49

- The teenager who does not come home on time on Friday night may lose the right to go out on Saturday night.

In all of these examples, we identify a consequence that is important to the child and then set the behavioral expectations according to this. It is not a natural consequence or something that automatically follows an activity, but it is a consequence that parents can create and individualize according to the interests, desires, and wishes of the particular adolescent.

Using Consequences to Change Behavior. Consequences are the most important aspects of behavior management. They are the primary determinates of whether a child will change his behavior and develop new behaviors. A child must consistently experience consequences in order to change.

The range of consequences that can be used dramatically decreases as the youngster enters adolescence. The nine-year-old will respond to numerous consequences. When this same child becomes thirteen, the number of important consequences starts decreasing, and oftentimes the range is very small. For the teenager, many of the important consequences center around money, cars, telephone, clothing, driving privileges, going out, more freedom, loosening of restrictions, and being treated like an adult. If the adolescent has a hobby (e.g., fishing, music), the range of important consequences may somewhat increase.

There are three major consequences that parents can use in dealing with their teenagers:

- Rewards, incentives, or positive consequences. If you see a behavior you like, reward it; that is, follow the behavior with some positive attention and something that is important or enjoyable to the child.

50

- Punishment or negative consequences. If you see a behavior you do not like, punish it; that is, follow the behavior with negative attention and something the child views as unenjoyable or by withdrawing something positive.

- Ignoring or no consequences. If you see a behavior you do not like, ignore it because maybe the attention you pay to it is the reason it exists. In other words, do not follow the behavior with either negative or positive attention.

Reward, punishment, and ignoring are the three major consequences that can be used in disciplining teenagers. These very important aspects of behavior management are described in detail in the following Keys.

11

▲▲

HOW TO BECOME A POSITIVE PARENT

There are three major consequences that can be used in dealing with teenage behavior, but the majority of parents usually rely primarily on one: punishment. Punishment means negative attention and emphasis on inappropriate behavior. The negative attention could involve anything from shouting to physical confrontation. Adults tend to stress the misbehaviors, mistakes, and faults of the teenager. Maybe this happens because this is the type of discipline we experienced or because society operates in that way or because some of the changes that occur in the typical adolescent provoke negative attention. Nevertheless, it happens.

Most professionals who are involved in behavior management and in providing parents with techniques to more effectively live and interact with as well as discipline their children stress a positive approach. They advise parents to shift the emphasis from what the child does wrong to what she does right. In this way, the parent will pay more attention to good behavior and less to inappropriate actions or misbehavior. The positive approach is primarily accomplished by using rewards, incentives, and positive consequences.

Determining what to use for a reward or an incentive can be easy in the case of some adolescents and more difficult in the case of others. The reward or incentive has to be individualized because what is important to one teenager might not be important to another. When trying to identify possible rewards, parents have to disregard their own values and what they feel is important and instead look closely at the teenager's interests, needs, and requests.

Types of Positive Consequences. A reward can be anything the adolescent regards as special. Some general areas follow:

- *Activity rewards or incentives.* These simply could be some type of activity that is important to the teenager. For example: Staying up past the normal bedtime. The parent paying for Internet services. Having someone sleep over. Extra phone time. Going to a concert. Practicing driving. Going to the mall with friends and without parents. Seeing a particular movie. More freedom. Fewer restrictions. Being treated more like an adult than a child. Using the car more frequently. Renting a video.

- *Material rewards or incentives.* These are usually concrete or material things that are of interest to the child: Extra spending money. Tires for the car. A new video game. An album. Clothes. Jewelry. Makeup. Parts for the bike.

- *Things you would usually get the child or allow him to do.* This category somewhat ties in with both activity rewards and material rewards. Sometimes when I talk with parents about using rewards and incentives, they say, "He gets that anyway" or "She does that already." Such a parent has difficulty finding a reward to use as a consequence because the child is receiving many rewards just for breathing! The other day when I discussed using sleeping at someone's house as an incentive for better school grades, the parent said, "I can't use that. Every Friday, either he sleeps at a friend's house or one of his friends sleeps at our house."

Many things that we buy our children, do for them, or allow them to do can instead be used as incentives and rewards. What we should try to do is to have them earn a reward, rather than have it just fall into their lap. In the above example, whether or not the child performed well in school, he was allowed to sleep over. It would be more effective if he had to earn this privilege by doing better in school. Then, whether he could sleep at a friend's house or have someone over each Friday would be totally his responsibility.

- *Social rewards or incentives.* This is the most powerful type of reward that parents have. It does not cost a penny and can be defined simply as praise, recognition, and positive attention for good behavior. While the range of material and activity rewards greatly decreases during adolescence, the range of social rewards does not. Social reward can be verbal approval, laughter, praise for doing a good job, a smile, a pat on the back, or other positive attention. In general, social reward is recognition of appropriate behavior—for example, for helping to set the table or for attention to everyday behaviors (picking up clothes, cleaning up after eating, coming home on time). It is telling your child how pleased with him or how proud of him you are. Social reward should also be used with both activity and material incentives. It is extremely important with adolescents because it increases the amount of positive interaction you have with your child.

12

REWARDS AND INCENTIVES: THINGS TO REMEMBER

Reward is a very powerful consequence and can be used to change behavior. However, several things must be kept in mind in order for a reward to work effectively.

The Reward Must Be Individualized. A consequence that is rewarding for one child may not have the same effect on another. See Keys 10 and 11 for further explanation.

A Social Reward Must Also Be Used. Regardless of the incentive (material or activity) used, a social reward—for example, praise—should always be paired with the behavior.

The Reward Should Not Occur Before the Desired Behavior. Parents often use rewards but make the mistake of rewarding the child before the desired behavior is seen. This is not a good way to use an incentive system. What would happen if you paid somebody to paint your house before the job was finished? It might end up half done or not completed to your satisfaction. The same thing can happen when you give a child a reward and then expect her to behave in a certain fashion. Reward should be based on behavior and should follow the expected actions. If it comes before the desired behavior, it may not work.

The Reward Earned Must Be Received. Often, teenagers earn behavior rewards but get them taken away because of some other negative behavior. This is a sure way to destroy the effectiveness of a reward system. Rewards earned must be received.

The Reward Should Be Given Immediately After the Desired Behavior. Ideally, if a child does something now, she should be rewarded immediately, not next week or next month. The effectiveness of a reward is, in part, based on how close it comes to the behavior you are trying to increase or control. How well a reward works is based not on quantity or expensiveness, but on frequency and immediacy. Therefore, rewards should be given often and as soon as possible.

It is not always possible to reward a child immediately for positive behavior with the desired incentives, but other types of rewards could be used. Let's say a child wants to obtain a driver's license but has been very uncooperative and argumentative at home. Rather than say, "If you behave the entire month, I'll take you to get your learner's permit," it might be better to say, "Each day that you cooperate and show a pleasant attitude around the house, I'll put a check on the calendar, and when you have twenty checks, I'll take you to get the learner's permit." Although obtaining the incentive or reward (permit) may be three or four weeks down the road, you can immediately reward the child on a daily basis for good behavior by awarding checks or points which in turn can be traded in for the desired incentive.

Improvement Should Be Rewarded. Often, a reward system does not work because parents expect too much change too rapidly and do not reward any improvement no matter how little. The child who is getting mainly D's and a few F's on her report cards is told that if she has a B average on the next report card, she will get a reward. The child who fights with his sister numerous times a day is told that if he does not fight all day today he will be able to earn a point toward a desired reward. In these examples, parents may be looking for too much change. In modifying a behavior, you should break it down into steps and look for gradual improvement. Movement toward a goal may be more important at first than actual attainment of the goal. A realistic goal for a D– student might be a D+ or C average, and an appropriate goal for the child who fights with his sister continuously might be to decrease the fighting by 30 percent.

In using rewards, the behavior or goals have to be broken down into steps, and small goals (gradual improvement) have to be rewarded. You cannot change a child's behavior 100 percent or overnight. You have to look at where the child is now and where you want him or her to go.

The Reward May Have to Be Changed. A reward's purpose is to change behavior. In most cases, interest and attitudes must also be modified. Therefore, a reward initially important to a child may lose its effectiveness with time and use. If a reward worked beautifully in the beginning but is no longer effective, it has to change because it has been used too much or too long.

Some rewards also can become part of the family rules. A child who earns a reward to stay up past her bedtime by cooperating may eventually have her bedtime extended anyway just because she is getting older. The child who initially used the car one night a week and then earned a second night by doing extra chores occasionally may eventually be able to use the car regularly twice a week because of his cooperativeness.

In addition, when first trying a reward, you should use it consistently for a time before you try another one because it is not working. Often a parent identifies an incentive that is important to the child, but because it does not work the first, second, or third time it is used, the parent then tries another one. Rewards need to be varied and changed, but not too quickly.

The Reward Should Be Attainable. When a reward system is first started, it should not be too complex or hard. The goal should not require a great deal of change and should be set up in such a way that the child succeeds and receives the reward. You have to lock the child into the system. If you make it too hard at first, the child is not able to attain the behavioral goal and incentive and your reward system will probably fail.

Expectations must be realistic so that the child will be able to attain the reward. A good rule to follow is to expect about a 30 to 40 percent change in the behavior at first.

If a reward system is made too complex or too difficult—that is, if too much work or change is required in order for the teenager to earn the reward—the child may think the reward is not worth the effort. For example, perhaps a parent decides that there are ten things a child must do each day to receive an allowance. Some teens may choose to go without money in that situation.

When you start a reward system, be sure your child will be able to achieve the reward fairly easily. This will increase the probability that future rewards will be effective and that change will occur.

13

TYPES OF PUNISHMENT

The same types of punishment that can be used with small children can also be used with adolescents. However, the number or range of punishments available to the parents of an adolescent dramatically decreases as the child gets older. The number of punishments available for an eight- or nine-year-old is much greater than those for a fifteen- or sixteen-year-old. In general, punishment can simply be defined as taking away or withholding something that is important to the adolescent or that will make an impact on him if he is denied it (a negative experience).

The types of punishment used by most parents can be grouped into five general areas. Some are effective and can be used frequently, while others are ineffective and should be used sparingly or avoided.

Loss of Privileges. This is often called *response cost* and is a very effective form of punishment. Under this system, the child is fined and/or loses privileges or desired activities for not completing certain tasks or for misbehavior. In other words, certain behaviors will cost the child certain things. Any type of activity, privilege, or thing that is important to the child can be used as the "fine" or consequence in this type of system.

An example may involve a child who has trouble coming home on time. She is always late and never arrives when told. A response cost system could be employed to change this behavior. The child would be told, "You're supposed to be home at ten. For the amount of time you are home later than ten, you will have to come home that much earlier tomorrow."

The child who continually talks back to her parents might be told that every time she does this or gives a smart aleck answer, a check will be placed on a sheet of paper on the refrigerator. For each check she receives that day, ten minutes of phone time will be deducted that night.

This is an effective form of punishment, but several points must be kept in mind when using this system. First, you have to clearly define the behavior that will be fined and exactly what it will cost the child. Second, the loss of privileges or the fines have to be consistently meted out when the misbehavior occurs. Third, it has been proven that this type of system works best when positive consequences or rewards are also being used. Fourth, do not set up a system where the loss will be unrealistic or where the child will owe you. For example, if you tell a recalcitrant teen that every time she talks back she will lose thirty minutes of phone time, she might be on the way to college before she regains phone privileges! Or if a parent tells a child, "For every A and B you get, I will give you a certain amount of money. However, for every D and F you get, you must give me a certain amount of money," at the end of the school year, the thirteen-year-old might owe more money than she has.

Removal from Pleasurable Activities. Often called *time-out punishment*, this is somewhat similar to "Go to your room" but involves much more than that consequence. For a time-out punishment to be effective, the child has to be engaged in some enjoyable or desired activity, from which this type of punishment will remove him. Because many children today have TVs, stereos, video games, computers, or other forms of entertainment in their rooms, being sent there may not be much of a penalty. In addition, since adolescents tend to spend a great deal of time in their room anyway, sending them there may not be an effective method of punishment.

Here is an example of a typical time-out punishment. A young girl who is out shopping with her mother for school clothes starts arguing loudly with her mother about the styles. The mother might tell her, "I'm going to give you a warning each time that you talk back to me. If we get to three warnings, we'll go home and postpone the shopping until next week." The message to the teen is that if she is unable to act appropriately in the store, she will be removed from it. Another example: You agree to go out for about thirty minutes with your sixteen-year-old so that he can practice driving the car. After a few minutes, he starts speeding. As a time-out punishment you might say, "For each time you exceed the speed limit the amount of time that we will be out here will be reduced by ten minutes."

The activity from which the child is "timed out" could be anything that is important to him. Several things must be kept in mind in order to make this technique successful. First, you have to make very clear what the child needs to do to merit the punishment. The behavior has to be identified and spelled out very clearly. For example, the parent might say, "I don't want to hear or see any more fighting. By that I mean hitting each other, name-calling, or teasing." Now the child knows exactly what behaviors will be followed by a time-out. Next, some type of warning should be given: "The next time I see you do that you will have to go to your room" or "I am going to give you three warnings and when we get to the third one, this is what will happen." The third thing to keep in mind is that the child should know how long he will be prohibited from the activity and what he must do to get out of the time-out. For example, the young girl who has been timed out from her shopping trip should <u>not</u> be told by her mother, "I will take you out shopping again when *I* decide to go." She should be given either a time period ("We will go shopping next week") or a specific behavior that must be performed or shown in order to re-earn the shopping trip ("If you cooperate around the house for three days without any more arguments, we will go shopping on Saturday").

The time-out procedure must be used consistently and may have to be employed several times in order to modify the behavior. Also, time-out punishment must be administered in a very matter-of-fact way without emotion; in other words, when the action is taken, the parent should not lecture, fuss, scold, get upset, nag, or apologize, but just follow through with the penalty that the child's behavior has called for.

Loss of Reward. When a reward system is used and the child does not receive the reward because he did not perform as desired, this can be viewed as a type of punishment. Oftentimes when I am designing a technique using reward to change behavior, parents will ask, "If he does not do what we want him to do, how do we punish him?" My answer is, "You do not have to punish him. That would be like using two barrels of a shotgun when you only need one. Save the punishment for some other type of behavior. Not receiving the reward can serve as the consequence."

Verbal Punishment. Yelling, screaming, criticizing, nagging, name-calling, and lecturing, as well as telling children things to make them feel guilty, embarrassed, or fearful are in this category. This is a very ineffective form of punishment, especially with adolescents. Many children learn to tune out and totally ignore their parents' ranting and raving. The scolding, lecturing, and shouting go in one ear and out the other. Some children develop resentment and anger toward the parents when these tactics are used, while others become more emotionally distant. Many of the problems described in Key 14 occur when verbal punishment is frequently used.

Physical Punishment. Hitting, slapping, spanking, or other physical acts like these fall in this category. It may also involve controlling the child through intimidation or fear. In other words, "I am bigger than you and, therefore, I can make you do what I want." I feel that numerous other forms of discipline can be used effectively with adolescents and that this form of punishment should be avoided.

14

∧∧

PROBLEMS WITH USING PUNISHMENT

Because of some of the normal changes that occur during adolescence (e.g., withdrawal from family activities, decrease in communication with parents, spending more time with friends), interaction between parent and teenager frequently decreases. In general, most parents tend to be punishers; that is, they tend to pay more attention to their children's mistakes, failures, and misbehaviors than to their accomplishments and successes. This attitude is somewhat amplified during the period of adolescence, and many teenagers complain that the only time their parents talk to them is to criticize, lecture, point out mistakes, or tell them what they should or should not do. Because of the decreasing interaction, the majority of parental communication involves negative attention or punishment.

By responding to teenagers in this negative fashion, parents set up a situation where the only reward the child receives for good behavior is to not be punished or criticized. Although you shouldn't always avoid using punishment or negative attention in disciplining or dealing with your teenager, *it is very important during adolescence to acknowledge positive behaviors and accomplishments.* Positive attention, rewarding, and ignoring should be the consequences used most of the time. When negative attention and punishment are the major methods of control or interaction, problems like the following may develop, and normal adolescent behaviors may become more intense.

The Child's Physical Size Will Approximate the Parent's, Preventing the Use of Certain Types of Discipline. Although aware of the fact that children physically develop as time passes, many of us tend to forget about this normal physical process when dealing with teenagers. Many forms of discipline used by parents are based on fear or intimidation. In other words, you can make children do things because you are bigger than them and can overpower or intimidate them. If this is the major method of control that has been used with the younger child, during adolescence parents are apt to lose control or get into some physical conflicts with the teen. This method may work well with younger children but is usually ineffective during adolescence, the time when you need more control than ever. Control by fear or intimidation should be avoided and is not an effective way of managing any child, but particularly an adolescent, because many teenagers are physically larger than their parents and do not fear them and/or may welcome a physical confrontation.

Anger, Stubbornness, and Rebellion May Intensify. As mentioned earlier, these are some of the typical behaviors that occur during adolescence. However, if the child receives an excessive amount of criticism and negative attention, these feelings and behaviors are apt to become more intense. Sometimes, underlying feelings of anger are expressed directly, but frequently this anger is expressed through a variety of passive-aggressive maneuvers, such as opposition, resistance, stubbornness, defiance, and rebellion. For instance, if you say something is black, the teen says that it's white or does the opposite of what you tell him to do. In addition, this anger may be displaced to other situations, and fighting with or showing anger toward siblings, peers, and/or other authority figures may be seen.

More Emotional Distance May Be Created Between Parent and Child. The normal process of adolescence includes some withdrawal from family involvement and closer ties with peers. Therefore, some emotional distance is automatically present between the child and the adult. However, if excessive punishment and/or negative attention is employed, this distance or separation may increase and ultimately result in a decrease in verbal interaction (only talking to the parent when necessary) and withdrawal (spending more time alone in his or her room, minimizing contact with the family). In general, more distance may be created between you and your adolescent.

Escape/Avoidance Behaviors May Develop. We all tend to avoid situations that produce negative attention. If every time you played golf the result was a negative experience or if every time you prepared a certain meal you received a lot of criticism or negative attention, you probably would find yourself avoiding the golf course or cooking that meal less and less. Adolescents often show the same feelings and behaviors when punishment or negative attention is the primary characteristic of their interaction with their parents; that is, they develop avoidance and escape behaviors. If every time a child cuts the grass all her mistakes are pointed out, she will quickly learn to avoid the job rather than correct the mistakes. If the subject of schoolwork or homework usually provokes yelling, fighting, lecturing, or other negative attention on the part of the parent, the child may tend to avoid the subject and to decrease the amount of time he spends on the work.

Lying, manipulating, running away from home, or not telling the whole truth are escape/avoidance behaviors that are frequently employed by adolescents experiencing these situations. When you see a child not telling the truth, trying to manipulate her parents, or using the ultimate escape behavior of running away, look at the type of consequence being used or the primary pattern of interaction with the child. If punishment/negative attention is the main method, this may be the reason for the behavior.

Punishment/Negative Attention May Not Work and May Actually Make the Situation Worse. As adults, you and I frequently read the personalities of our friends and other adults and then deal with them accordingly. This skill is often lost or ignored when it comes to dealing with our children. For some personality types, punishment is sufficient to control or modify behavior. But for other personality types, punishment or negative attention either does not work at all, works only for a short period of time, or makes matters worse. This is especially true for stubborn, strong-willed, and pleasure-oriented personalities. In these instances, other consequences (rewarding and ignoring) must be used, because punishment as a main method of control will not be effective.

Anger, Opposition, and Rebellion Are More Likely to Be Expressed During Adolescence. When negative attention, criticism, fear, or punishment is the main method of discipline used in the home, children with certain personality characteristics often develop model behaviors when they are young. These youngsters, who seem to be "too good to be true," always listen, never give their parents any trouble, and are very compliant. If told to stand in a corner for an hour without moving, they would probably do so. However, somewhere between eleven and fourteen years of age, this compliant behavior dramatically changes. It is as if the child is no longer fearful, as if the anger that has been developing for years suddenly surfaces and is being expressed through some of the passive-aggressive methods described earlier.

The Child May Act Like You! My response to parents who tell me "Every time I hit my son, he hits me back. What should I do?" or "Every time I yell at my daughter, she yells back" is "Don't hit your son" or "Don't yell at your daughter." Children learn behaviors by observing other people. This is called the *modeling theory of learning.* In other words, parents serve as a model for children's behavior. Children exposed to certain behaviors will imitate them and may incorporate them into their patterns of dealing with conflicts, solving problems, and interacting with others.

If you frequently communicate with your children or spouse by shouting, arguing, or screaming, your child may be learning to deal in the same way with you, his siblings, or his peers. If you use physical control, fear, and intimidation to control your teenagers, they may start using these techniques on you. Most children who show aggressive behaviors have seen this negative method of problem solving modeled by their parents and/or have had it used on them.

Probably the most overused comment in explaining or analyzing the reason children do certain things is "They're doing it to get attention." While "getting attention" is frequently used inaccurately to explain certain behaviors in children, this statement is sometimes true, especially in adolescents. It is not so much that the child is behaving to get the negative attention but is acting in certain ways to get a certain reaction from the parents. Opposition, stubbornness, resistance, and mumbling under the breath are passive-aggressive methods of expressing anger.

Misbehaving in certain ways to get a reaction from parents is sometimes not consciously planned, but frequently adolescents say or do certain things primarily to provoke a reaction. One method of dealing with this type of behavior is to ignore it. (See Keys 16 and 17.) Key 21 also gives some tips on dealing with this type of behavior.

68

15

~~~~~~

USING PUNISHMENT: THINGS TO REMEMBER

Punishment is a consequence that can be used to change behavior. However, there are several things that must be kept in mind to make punishment work effectively and to minimize the occurrence of problems.

Use with Other Consequences. Three major consequences can be used in discipline: punishment, reward, and ignoring. Punishment is more effective when it is used with one of the other consequences. When it is used as the main method of control, it is less effective than when it is used in conjunction with reward. Losing privileges or being restricted from desired activities is more effective if the child earns rewards and privileges for other behaviors. The more reward, praise, or positive attention that is employed, the more effective the punishment system.

Define Expectations and Rules. This was discussed earlier in Keys 9 and 10. Basically, parents should avoid ambiguous remarks such as "I want you to be good (behave, improve in school)" and state exactly what they mean by "good" or "behave." Parents should also avoid random punishment; they should not decide the punishment *after* the rule is broken. The negative consequence should be spelled out along with the rule before the behavior occurs.

Tell the Child What Must Be Done for the Punishment to End. When punished, children should know how long the penalty is to last and/or what to do to escape punishment. For example, you might forbid telephone use for one week. That clearly defines the length of time. Or you might say, "You cannot talk on the phone for two days, but, after that, every afternoon you come home and do your homework without an argument, you can use the phone after dinner." This allows the child to know exactly what has to be done to get out of the punishment.

You must clearly define the behavior to be punished, state the negative consequence ahead of time with the rule, and tell the child how long he will be punished and/or what behavior he must show to get out of the punishment.

Try to Set the Rule and the Consequence the First Time You See the Behavior. In other words, try to avoid punishing a behavior the first time it appears, but use it to set a rule. This cannot be done all of the time, but this principle usually can be employed. For example, a teenager who has been consistently punctual suddenly comes home an hour late. Rather than punish the behavior the first time, you would use this to set a rule and a consequence by telling the child this is unacceptable behavior and the next time it occurs such and such will happen.

Use Signals or Warnings. Most parents do use signals or warnings, but often these involve negative reactions such as screaming, nagging, or getting upset. The use of appropriate signals and warnings can make things run smoother and eliminate a significant amount of hassle.

Events in the environment can serve as signals. "I would like the grass cut by 7:00 P.M. Saturday." The time and day become the signal. "I want this room cleaned up before your favorite program begins." "The garbage has to be put out after we eat dinner." Parents can let events or cues in the environment warn the child, and not use their voices as the signal.

Counting to three, giving three warnings, or using "The next time that happens . . ." or some other verbal statement in a matter-of-fact fashion can also serve as an effective signal.

Use signals to create a buffer period and avoid the situation that occurs when you say, "I want it done now, right now." Rather than demand, "I want the clothes folded right now," you might say, "I would like the clothes folded before dinner." Or "Your room has to be cleaned by five o'clock on Friday for you to get your allowance." This gives the child some flexibility, allowing her some time to get the job accomplished. If she does not finish the task by the signaled time, then a consequence should follow. Giving her a signal to serve as a buffer period might also reduce some of the normal teen resistance to parental demands.

Individualize the Punishment. As discussed in Key 11, when deciding on a negative consequence, the interests, values, and preferences of the child must be considered. What may be a punishment for one child may not be a negative consequence for another.

Punish the Behavior, Not the Child. When you use punishment, you should comment on the behavior and not on the child as an individual. If a child fails a test in school, this does not mean she is stupid. It probably means that she did not adequately prepare for the test. If a child hits his brother, this action does not necessarily suggest he is mean. It is the behavior that is unacceptable.

Stay Calm. This is much easier said than done, but whenever punishment is administered, parents should try to remain calm, cool, and collected. The behavior being dealt

71

with should be treated in a very matter-of-fact fashion. If a child loses a privilege, the parents should avoid excessive nagging, scolding, or lecturing, but simply follow through with the consequence of his behavior.

Do Not Overuse a Punishment. Parents should limit specific punishments to specific behaviors. As an example, loss of car privileges should be used only for certain behaviors and not for every violation of parental rules. If a child is restricted from the phone for a number of different behaviors, pretty soon not talking on the phone becomes a way of life and the punishment loses its effectiveness.

Try to Punish Immediately. In general, the importance or effectiveness of punishment primarily depends on how close it occurs to the behavior you are trying to control or change and not on the harshness or length of the punishment.

Punishment Does Not Have to Be Harsh or Lengthy to Be Effective. One of the main factors that control or change behavior is not the major or severe consequences that only occur every now and then, but the small consequences that follow a behavior response each time it appears.

One good rule of thumb to keep in mind when trying to determine how long to punish your child is to watch him closely and see how he reacts. See how long it takes before he occupies himself with something and/or appears to care less about the punishment. The punishment's effectiveness is primarily determined by how closely it follows the behavior and how frequently punishment occurs. (For more on this topic, see Key 24.)

16

~~~~~~

IGNORING CERTAIN BEHAVIORS

Some adolescent behaviors exist because of the reactions given to them by parents. Some teenagers realize that complaining, insolence, mumbling under their breath, and temper outbursts will provoke a reaction from parents and/or will get them what they want. Behaviors like these are often exhibited because of the consequence that the child receives for the behavior. All behavior exists for a reason, and in order to eliminate some types of behavior, it is necessary to remove the consequence (the parental response of lecturing, screaming, nagging, getting upset, or giving in to the child)—in other words, to ignore the negative behavior. Ignoring undesirable actions is a powerful method of discipline, but most of us do not use it too frequently because it is hard to do. Also, there are only certain behaviors where ignoring will work effectively.

What to Ignore. Ignoring or providing no consequences changes or eliminates only certain behaviors. On others, it has no effect. The obvious question is what should or should not be ignored?

You should not ignore behaviors that disrupt the activities of others, that may lead to injury to others or damage to property, or that cause neglect in performing a duty. Examples are leaving clothes all over the house, hitting a sibling, failing to perform household duties or do homework, or similar behaviors. Positive or negative consequences should be employed to deal with these.

To determine what behaviors should be ignored, you should first analyze the action and ask several questions: What is the child getting out of the behavior? Why is he doing this? What is the purpose of the behavior? If the answer is "He's getting me upset," "He's making me yell and scream," "He's getting a lecture," "I get nervous," "We get into a power struggle or screaming match," "I cry or leave him alone," "I give in to him," or "He gets his way," then this is the type of behavior that should be ignored. Removing consequences can be a very effective method in changing or eliminating behaviors that are primarily intended to provoke a reaction from the parents or get the child what he wants.

Let's say you ask your teenager to fold the clean laundry. While doing it, she starts mumbling under her breath. Most of what she says, you cannot understand, but every now and then you hear something like, "They think I'm a slave around here. These aren't all my clothes. Why do I have to fold them for everyone? They're always making me do stuff. My brother never has to do anything." Although she is folding the wash as you have asked, you get annoyed and start reacting to the mumbling: "Speak up. What are you saying? You live in this house and you have duties too. Stop mumbling." With each statement your voice gets louder and louder and you become more upset. Probably the main reason that the child's mumbling continues is your reaction to it. Therefore, it should be ignored. A similar situation may occur when parents ground a child or make him do something that he doesn't want to do. If the behavior is ignored and the adolescent does not get a response from the parents, this type of behavior usually diminishes, because it does not serve a purpose.

Manipulative behaviors (asking a lot of questions, refusing to take no for an answer, persistent pleading) that are designed to get the child what he wants should be ignored. If a child asks, "Can I go to the concert?" and the parent says, "No," then the manipulative teenager may begin, "You never let me go anyplace. Everybody in my class is going. I'm the only one that will be staying home. Everyone will think I'm a baby." After a while, the parent grows tired of the tirade and agrees to let the child go. Oftentimes, teenagers wear down their parents with continual pleading or questions and finally get their way. If this behavior is ignored and the child does not get what he wants, it will usually diminish.

How to Ignore. Ignoring the types of behaviors described above usually produces behavioral changes, but this procedure has to be employed consistently. There are two ways to ignore. One is difficult, the other much easier.

The difficult method of ignoring involves withdrawing all attention from the behavior. In other words, you must pretend that the behavior does not exist or that the child is not there. There should be no talking to the child, no facial or gestural indications of disapproval, no mumbling to yourself. You have to withdraw all attention. Using the example of the child who mumbles as she folds up the laundry, you would pretend she is not even in the room or you do not hear what she is saying. This type of ignoring can be used with some adolescent behaviors.

The second type of ignoring, which is somewhat easier and probably should be used more frequently, is one in which you withdraw emotional attention from the child's behavior, but still deal with the behavior. With this type of ignoring, the shouting, verbal reprimands, and emotional attention by the parent are eliminated; however, some disciplinary action is taken. For example, if you tell a child he cannot go to a concert and he persists in begging, you might say, "I don't want to hear any more. If you keep it up, I'm going to give you a warning. And for every warning you get, there will be additional restrictions for the weekend." In the previous example of a child asking to go to a concert, it was more to the child's advantage to keep aggravating the parent, because he eventually would get what he wanted. In this example, however, it is more of a disadvantage to keep annoying the parent because the additional questioning will not get the teen what he wants and will only get him deeper and deeper in a hole in terms of more restrictions. Therefore, it is important for a parent to deal with the negative behavior and to administer the consequence in a matter-of-fact manner, not getting upset or telling the child to stop or threatening him.

Behavioral problems like being flippant, talking back, or wrangling with siblings could be dealt with in a similar way. When the identified behavior is seen or heard, the parent should stay calm and carry out the consequence that was previously determined. No emotional attention is given to the behavior by the parent and/or the child does not get what he wants.

17

▼▼▼

IGNORING: THINGS
TO REMEMBER

Be Consistent. It is extremely important to be consistent when the disciplinary consequence of ignoring is chosen to deal with a certain behavior. If you decided to ignore your teen's complaining or mumbling, you must do it every time the behavior occurs. You cannot ignore it one time, then attend to it the next, and then go back to ignoring it, because your vacillation may be sufficient incentive to keep the behavior going.

Be Sure the Behavior Is Actually Being Ignored. Many times when parents think they are ignoring the behavior, they are not totally eliminating *all* the attention or consequences. Therefore, when this method of disciplining is used, be sure that all reactions—verbal (e.g., lecturing, shouting, mumbling under your breath) and nonverbal (e.g., glaring angrily, rolling your eyes, shaking your head, slamming the door)—are withheld in regard to your child's undesirable behavior.

Continue Ignoring the Behavior Even If It Gets Worse. Sometimes when the attention or consequence that is usually given for a behavior is withdrawn, the behavior may get worse or intensify before it gets better. The child who usually can annoy his mother for ten minutes and then succeed in getting what he wants may continue this behavior for fifteen, twenty, thirty minutes or even longer when it is at first ignored. In other words, since the behavior that usually gets him what he wants no longer works right away, he may persist with louder and louder complaints. However, after a while when he realizes this behavior serves no purpose, it should start to decrease in frequency and intensity.

Until he realizes the behavior is fruitless, a child will periodically test his parents to see if they will stick to their guns. Therefore, when the behavior gets worse, it is important that the parents continue to withdraw the emotional attention.

Ignore First, Then Use Other Consequences. For the behaviors described above, a good rule to keep in mind is to try to use the consequence of ignoring first in an attempt to eliminate them. This tactic will usually produce successful results on behaviors whose primary purpose is to provoke a reaction from the parent and/or get the child what he wants. However, in some cases, ignoring will not be sufficient to change the behavior. In these situations, positive or negative consequences must next be employed when the ignored behavior does not improve.

18

^^^

INCREASING COMMUNICATION BETWEEN PARENT AND TEENAGER

Communication with the teenager is extremely important, but many of the typical changes that occur during adolescence tend to interfere with the effectiveness and amount of interaction between parent and child. Although adults have much more experience in life than the adolescent, the teen is usually not aware of this fact or does not believe it; therefore, the advice, wisdom, and directions of parents are often not valued. Teens tend to spend more time in their room, with their peers, and away from family activities. Consequently, opportunities for communication diminish during this period of the child's life.

Because of these and other factors during adolescence, children do not confide in us as readily or communicate their feelings as much as they did when they were younger. In addition, general communication about their activities—what they did the day before, where they are going, or whom they are going with—also decreases. Therefore, many parents of teenagers have problems talking to their children, giving them advice, knowing their true feelings, or explaining things to them. On the other hand, children may have difficulty talking to their parents, expressing opinions, discussing things that bother them, or relating their experiences. These difficulties with verbal interaction are generally termed *lack of communication*. Communication problems may be described in a variety of ways.

A parent might say:

- My son is always on the phone, sleeping, out with his friends, or in his room. He never has time to talk to me.
- Every time I try to explain something to my daughter or give her advice, she gets upset and storms out of the room.
- When I talk to my child, he gives me a blank stare and is obviously not listening to anything I am saying.
- My youngest one never tells me when something is bothering her. I never know how she is feeling. She keeps everything to herself.
- If I ask my son a simple question like "How was your day?" he gets irritated and gives me a sharp answer. I can't even talk to him about simple things like his daily activities.

On the other hand, the adolescent might say:

- They're always asking me questions. Where did you go? Who did you go with? Did you have fun? It's like a third degree. When my friends come over, my parents even ask them a bunch of stupid questions too, like "Where do you go to school?" or "Where does your dad work?"
- My parents don't understand me. They are living in another time period.
- The only time my father talks to me is when I do something wrong or when he's trying to point out what I should do.
- It seems as though every time I tell my parents what my opinion is or how I feel, they tell me how wrong I am or why I shouldn't feel that way.

- Every time I ask my parents something, I get a lecture.
- My mother is always talking and I can't get a word in. She asks me a question and then gives me the answer.

Communication problems are numerous and varied. Some of the things that interfere with effective communication with your child and some suggestions that will increase the quantity and improve the quality of communication between you and your teenager are discussed in this next part. By using some of these concepts it should become easier for you to talk with your child, and the resulting verbal interaction should increase in frequency and grow more meaningful.

Opportunities for Communication Must Be Available. If you are in New York City and I am in New Orleans, the odds that we will communicate often or at length are slim. Similarly, if your teenager spends most of the time in his room and you keep busy in another part of the house, the odds are also slim that there will be much interaction between you and your adolescent. Therefore, before any form of communication can occur, you and your child must be together in the same room or location. You need to create opportunities for communication. The suggestions that follow are designed to increase both the amount of communication and your teenager's desire to communicate with you.

If your teenager does not drive or is too young to have a license, and if, as a result, you have to transport him to various places (e.g., to a friend's house, a football game, a doctor's appointment), the time you spend together in the car may be an opportune moment for communication. Another suggestion is to get more involved in activities that are of interest to the adolescent: help him wash or work on his car; go shopping with him; play golf, go fishing, or become

81

involved in leisure activities consistent with his interests. You might even want to visit his room (if you can find a place to sit) and listen to the music he likes and discuss that with him. Perhaps your daughter is interested in cooking or your son in how to build or repair things and these activities could be used as opportunities for communication. Although teenagers probably will not accept your invitation, you could ask if they want to accompany you to visit their aunt or their grandparents, go out to eat, or take in a movie. Most of the time they will decline because they would rather be doing something else or be with their friends, but they might surprise you and agree. The chance that they will come with you may increase if you tell them they can bring a friend, but don't count on this happening.

Try to provide as many opportunities as possible for you and your teenager to be together so communication can occur.

Talk Just to Be Talking. Because communication between parents and children decreases with the advent of adolescence, much of the verbal interaction that we do have with the youngsters is designed to get a point across, teach them something, get them to see the situation from a different angle, change their attitude, tell them what they are doing wrong, show them how to do it correctly, or convince them of the importance of certain activities. In other words, when we talk to them, we are trying to accomplish something more than a simple, enjoyable conversation. If this is the majority of communication that we have with our teenagers, their willingness to talk to us will certainly decrease. An important goal in communicating with teens should be just talking with them without trying to accomplish anything other than talking.

This can primarily be achieved by discussing with the teenager something that is of interest to him or her. Some of my children's interests at the current time center around sports, skateboards, cars, music, and the opposite sex. If I want to have a conversation with them just to talk, and for no other purpose, this can usually be accomplished by discussing one of the above subjects. You can speak with your youngsters about movies they have seen, TV programs, rock stars, school news, and other subjects you know will interest them. Many times it is important just to communicate with them, without trying to accomplish anything, make a point, or get them to understand a concept. Talk just to talk.

Some teenagers tell me that when they talk to their parents about various things, the conversation usually ends up in lectures or preaching. In other words, the child may say, "When I'm talking with them just to have a conversation, they use what I say either to make a point, to teach me something, or to explain certain things." Often when this is the case, a child will stop communicating. A case in point is that of the sixteen-year-old who is talking to his mother about a friend who quit school. "Mom, Mike has been working at the fast-food restaurant since he stopped going to school. He really hates the job and says it's a lot of work and he doesn't get paid much money. He's thinking about quitting and finding another job." Instead of listening to her son and taking this opportunity to talk to him about what he is saying, the mother uses his remarks as a launching pad to discuss the value of education—why he should stay in school, how he will need an education to get a good job, and so on. The child started the conversation to have some verbal interchange and what resulted was a lecture he did not want to hear. In another example, a girl is talking to her mother about a friend's sixteen-year-old cousin who already has a baby and is pregnant again. This information results in a lecture on sex, boys, the need to be careful, and other bits of advice. In these two instances, the children are talking to their parents just to talk, but instead they receive Lecture 101. When teenagers attempt to converse with their parents and get this type of response, communication with parents will decrease.

Try to Be Positive. As mentioned, much of our interaction with the adolescent involves correction or trying to teach something, get a point across, or change an attitude. Therefore, much of the communication is often negative. Parents frequently pay more attention to mistakes, misbehaviors, and failures than they do to successes and accomplishments. This is especially true in adolescence. A teenager whose job is to walk the dog before bedtime does this six nights in a row, but forgets on the seventh night. When does she get attention for this behavior? Usually on the one night she forgets to walk the dog! Nobody says anything complimentary about her performance on the other six nights. Another example: Your son cleans the kitchen and does a beautiful job, except that he forgets to empty the dishwasher. Of course, the attention for cleaning the kitchen will focus on the one chore that was overlooked. Another child does an excellent job cutting the grass, edging, and sweeping, but fails to put the gasoline can back in the garage. The good behavior is overlooked and the emphasis is on the can of gas that was left out.

Would you frequently communicate with or become fond of a boss who is constantly critical of your performance? No, you would tend to avoid that person and keep your verbal interaction to a minimum. All of us try to avoid situations that produce negative attention. Therefore, if the majority of your verbal interaction with the adolescent is negative, she will try to avoid it. The end result will be that the amount of time she spends talking to you will be reduced. Think about the last ten discussions or verbal interactions you had with your adolescent. Did most of them involve some type of correction or discussion that empha-sized what the child was doing wrong, her negative behavior, or what she should or should not do?

Although most parents find it easier to praise a young child than an adolescent, you should pay attention to some of the teen's appropriate behaviors when they occur (e.g., when the clothes are put away or when the cat's litter box is changed). If 99 percent of the kitchen has been cleaned and only one percent is dirty, you should offer 99 percent posi-tive attention and either overlook the negative or sandwich it somewhere in your positive response to the appropriate behavior. Work at increasing positive verbal interaction.

Communicate with the teenager about his successes, accomplishments, and good behaviors as much or more than you talk to him about his failures, mistakes, and bad behav-iors. If you interacted with your child three times today and all three occasions were negative, this is worse than if you interacted with him 100 times today, and fifty occasions were negative and fifty positive. In general, a good rule of thumb to keep in mind is that when you get ready to go to bed and review your day with the child, you want to be sure you have spent more time looking at positive behaviors, attitudes, and activities than you have spent looking at negative behaviors. Teenagers who receive a significant amount of positive ver-bal attention and interaction want to talk more with their parents. If this occurs, the lines of communication will be kept open and you will become more aware of your teenager's feelings, opinions, and objections.

You Can Talk Too Much. Some parents just talk too much. For example: A child asks her father to help with an algebra problem because she has run into difficulty with a particular step. The father sits down and spends forty-five minutes explaining things like unknown values, rational coefficients, and extraction of roots. The teenager then thinks, "When I ask my parents to help me with homework, all I want them to do is answer a particular question, which will probably take a minute or two, and instead they sit down and spend an hour trying to get me to understand the whole concept of the subject." The result is that this adolescent stops asking her parents to help with homework.

There are several different areas where parents tend to talk too much.

Questions. The average teenager does not like to be asked many questions. Even simple, casual questions, such as "How was your day?" "Did you have a good time last night?" "Where are you going Saturday?" are sometimes seen as the third degree. Many times adolescents who experience a lot of questions will respond with flippant answers, will tell the parent exactly what he or she wants to hear, or will not respond at all.

Rather than ask the teenager a complex series of questions or put her through the third degree, a parent is better advised to discuss the situation with the teenager. Talk to her about what has happened and go with the flow of the conversation rather than put her on the spot or ask her a number of disjointed questions. For example, your son has just started a new friendship and you want to know something about the friend and his family. Rather than ask a series of questions such as "How old is Johnny?" "Where does he go to school?" "Does he have any brothers or sisters?" "Where does his father work?" you could ask one question or wait for the child to start talking about his friend and then sit down and listen. The teenager's response to the one question may offer a variety of information or his conversation may provide you with several areas to pursue. For example, you might ask, "What did you do at Johnny's house today?" or he might just

86

volunteer that information. While discussing what he and Johnny did, your child may generate some other information like "Johnny's brother came with us to pick up a tape at Billy's house." You could then use the mention of the brother to ask about Johnny's siblings. Other responses by your son might mention Johnny's parents, schooling, or some other aspects. The information provided by your son will help you to determine the direction of the conversation. By responding to the child in this fashion, it does not seem as if a series of questions is being directed at the adolescent and, as a result, the conversation flows more smoothly. Try to avoid disjointed questions and use the information supplied by your child to direct the flow of the conversation and to gather the knowledge that you desire.

Some children complain, "My mother asks me a question and then answers it herself before I have time to say anything." This type of response by a parent is a good way to minimize communication between parent and child. You have to be a good listener and give your child an opportunity to respond to your questions.

Lectures. "Oh, no. Here comes Lecture 35 again." Some children tell me their parents should put some of their lectures on tape and just replay them, because they have heard them so many times before. One child told me that he hates to have discussions with his father. When I asked him why, he said, "Every time I do something wrong or get a bad grade from school, my father sits down and has a long talk with me." In other words, much of the father's interaction with this child involves lectures.

Sometimes when we are trying to make a point with a youngster, it is best to be brief rather than to provide another lecture. Children usually tune out lectures. Your communication will be more effective if you are brief and to the point.

Repetition. This topic involves both of the above areas (questions and lectures) as well as some others. Parents tend to give the same lecture over and over again and sometimes ask the same question repeatedly. This is a good way to turn off the kids and minimize verbal interaction. Repetition also involves nagging: "Did you do your homework?" may be asked several times a day. Instructions like "Go clean your room" are repeated too many times.

Most of the time, parents continually repeat things because the teen does not do what they request. As mentioned earlier, rather than remind a child 500 times to clean his or her room, it would be better to set a rule and the consequence of the behavior. Spell out what you expect and what will happen; then leave it alone. "You cannot go out Saturday night until you clean your room." "You cannot talk on the phone until your homework is completed."

Excessive questioning, lectures, and repetition of questions and instructions produce more anger, resentment, stubbornness, opposition, and back talk. Remember, teenagers are often already annoyed with these "stupid grownups" for telling them to do something. The more that this negative type of interaction exists, the more likely it is that anger, resentment, and other negative feelings will develop.

Talk Sometimes Does Not Change Behavior. For some teenagers, talk, explanations, lectures, conversations, or trying to get them to see the problem from a different angle will help to change their behavior. For others, the talk is about as effective as asking the wall to move back four feet and will not work to change the behavior. This is explained in detail in Key 23. Some children, "attitude kids," develop appropriate attitudes through communication or explanation. Once they have developed the desired attitude, their behavior will change. For other teenagers, talk, explanations, and lectures go in one ear and out the other and will not change their behavior. These children need to experience consequences and by experiencing the consequences of their behavior, they develop the desired attitude. Therefore, talk and verbal interaction with some children should be used as a form of communication, not as a disciplinary tactic to change behavior. For these youngsters, what you say is not as important as what you do.

Let us use as an example the fifteen-year-old who is continually hitting his younger brother, who weighs sixty pounds less. The parent sits down with the older boy and explains carefully how he can hurt his brother, how his brother is much smaller, how he should tolerate his brother, how he should love his brother, and how he should not hit him. However, after numerous repetitions of this explanation, the child still continues to hit his little brother.

Another child who is not doing homework has received at least forty-seven different lectures on the importance of education and the need to do homework, but still appears to have an "I don't care" attitude when it comes to school-related work.

Excessive explaining to this type of child will only interfere with effective communication. In the examples above, the parent should say, "The next time you hit your brother, this [consequence] is going to happen to you, and if you don't hit your brother, something different [a different consequence] is going to happen to you." Or "If you do your homework, you will be able to use the car this weekend or go to the movies on Saturday. The week you do not do your homework, you will not be able to go out on the weekend."

Think Before You Open Your Mouth. This topic primarily involves overreacting to what has been said by an adolescent or reacting to him before you have a chance to think. Many times teenagers say things just to get parents upset or to get a reaction from them. When you overreact, you are giving them exactly what they want. If this occurs, they may continue to say things that provoke a reaction. A fifteen-year-old may say, "I'm quitting school. I don't need an education. I'm tired of all of this homework." The parent may then overreact, get upset, start lecturing and berating the youngster, pointing out the value of education. Another child who does not get her way may say, "I'm leaving this house and never coming back." Again, an overreaction frequently follows a statement like this.

The other reaction that falls in this category involves not thinking before you respond to a child. It may be something as simple as this: A child asks his parent, "Mom, can I sleep at Robbie's house?" A second after the child asks the question, the mother says, "No." After thinking about it for a while, she realizes that there was no reason to say no and now tells him he can go. Some parents will respond negatively before they have a chance even to think about the question.

My son had a summer job, and after working two weeks and receiving his first paycheck, he told me he was going to buy a new car. My initial thoughts were, "You have to be crazy. You don't even have enough money to buy a set of tires. Do you know how much a new car costs?" In other words, I wanted to tell him how crazy and impossible the idea was. Rather than respond in this fashion, however, I just began to talk to him about the type of car he was going to buy, the color of the car, and so on. After a while, we got into a discussion of how much the car would cost, and I think he began to realize how far he had to go before he could even consider getting a new car. In other words, I think he then realized what I initially thought without my having to say it.

A significant amount of negative attention, confrontation, explaining away a child's feelings, or telling him how wrong he is can be avoided by staying calm and thinking a little before you talk. This is much easier said than done but usually becomes less difficult with practice. Rather than react or overreact to the child, talk to him. If you have assessed the situation and feel that the reason that your child is saying certain things is to get a reaction from you, do not give him the reaction. If you have a tendency to overreact or to respond to your child before thinking, it might be a good idea to tell him that you will consider the situation, or use the "Let me think about it and I'll get back to you later" approach. Then after a period of time, you can talk to him. You could also tell him that you want to discuss this matter with your spouse and will get back to him. Be sure you do get back to him later. Counting to ten and various other techniques can also be used to help you think before you respond.

"Because I Said So." Although we are generally trying to understand the adolescent's feelings and to communicate effectively with him or her, there are some situations where your only response may be "Do it because I said so." This is especially true if you have a child who cannot take no for an answer. You could give a hundred explanations for denying his request, but the only answer that he wants to hear is "yes" to his demand. Any other answer will fall on deaf ears, and reasoning, discussions, or explanations are fruitless.

Suppose I tell you that I feel I should be able to work three-and-a-half days a week and be off three-and-a-half days. After I make this statement, you respond by explaining, "People used to work seven days a week. You should be happy you're only working five. In fact, you should be grateful to have a job." However, the only explanation that will really satisfy me is for you to say, "You're absolutely right. Go

91

ahead and work just three-and-a-half days." However, if I were working for you, you would probably tell me, "I'm the boss and you're the employee. You either come to work five days a week or look for another job." In other words, the reason that applies here is "Because I said so." Another example: "Give me a good reason for making the bed every day if I'm going to mess it up every night." The parent may not have a good reason for this question other than "This is my house. I have the job, I pay the bills, and as long as you're living here, you'll do it because I said so."

This method of communication should not be used frequently. However, if you have a teenager who is always demanding numerous explanations and the only thing that will satisfy him is to agree with him or tell him what he wants to hear, you may have to resort to the "Because I said so" technique.

Not "Why?" But "What Can I Do?" This is a concept I frequently discuss with teenagers who tell me, "My parents don't understand my side of the story. They won't listen to me. I don't know what I have to do to earn this privilege I want." Often when a teenager asks "Why?" it results in an explanation from the parent and the above feelings for the child. The child asks "Why?" again and the parent gives another explanation. After a while, both parent and teen become frustrated.

Suppose a teenager with a 12:30 A.M. curfew asks his father to increase it to 1:00 A.M., but the parent refuses. When the teenager asks why, the parent says, "There is nothing you can do after 12:30 at night except get into trouble." The child responds, "All my friends are staying out, so why can't I?" and another explanation follows. After numerous explanations, he is still asking why and the parent is still telling him, "Because I cannot trust you. You are not responsible. You

92

may not go where you tell us you're going. I'm worried about you." At the end of all the discussion, the child still is not able to stay out later. Rather than have the teenager continually ask why, I suggest he try, "What can I do to earn this privilege?" If a parent says, "No, you cannot stay out past 12:30 because I don't feel you are responsible enough or I can't trust you," a response by the adolescent that would increase communication and move toward a compromise would be, "What can I do to show you that I am responsible so that I can have this privilege?" In other words, "What behaviors must I display in order for you to develop more confidence in my responsibility?" Parent response to this question might include such things as more involvement in schoolwork, a decrease in lying, or more cooperation around the house. The teenager now has an idea of what he has to do to achieve this specific goal. By responding in this way, both parent and teenager set up a situation for a compromise. If a child gives his parents what they ask for, he will be able to get what he requests. I often tell the teenager that "Why?" will get him nothing, but that "What can I do?" may get him something he wants.

19

^^

LEARNING TO LISTEN AND TO UNDERSTAND

Listen. In order to communicate effectively with another individual, you must *listen* to what he or she is saying—a lot easier said than done. Many people have difficulty listening to others. On the other hand, when communicating with other people, some individuals have learned to focus on what the person is saying.

Suppose that you and I are discussing the current president of the United States. I feel that he is the best president we have ever had. You totally disagree and feel that he is the worst one we have ever had. In the discussion that follows, you ask, "Why do you think he is the most important or best president?" I then give you a list of reasons, as well as some of the important things that he has done. Rather than tying to explain how I'm wrong or thinking up arguments about what I've said, you should try to listen to me and try to understand my position. In other words, the listener should try to hear and understand where the other person is coming from, and not prepare arguments or retaliations. The individual who is really listening tends not to interrupt and give her own point of view, but rather will ask additional questions in order to clarify and understand the other person's position.

Give Them Your Attention. Because adolescents do not frequently volunteer information or initiate conversations with us, we should give them our undivided attention

94

when this desired communication does occur. You and I would not talk to people who ignore us or appear disinterested when we try to communicate with them. If parents seem uncaring about or inattentive to what the teenager has to say, attempts to volunteer information or communicate will diminish.

A child comes home from a day at school during which a great deal has happened and she has quite a bit to tell her mother. When she finds that her mother is busy preparing dinner, she sits down at the kitchen table and starts talking to the mother. The mother does answer, but because she continues cooking, the teenager must talk to the back of her head. Would you continue to communicate with someone if you had to talk to the back of her head?

Another child tries to talk to his father, who has his head buried in the newspaper. The child makes several attempts to strike up a conversation, but gets tired talking to the newspaper and stops.

One sure way to minimize the verbal interaction between you and your teenager is to respond to him or her in ways similar to those just described. In order to keep children talking and increase the probability that they will easily communicate their feelings to you, you must give them your full attention. When a child has something to tell you, put down the newspaper, stop cooking (if possible), turn off the television, sit down, look the child in the eyes, and listen to him. Take a few minutes to stop what you are doing and give him your undivided attention. No one likes to talk if the other party appears disinterested or is involved in another activity.

Try to Understand Their Feelings. Many times when a teenager comes to us and expresses his feelings, opinions, or attitudes concerning a certain subject, we try to explain away these feelings, fix the situation, and make the child feel better. We try to convince him that the way he feels is inappropriate or incorrect. This is a typical parental reaction. A teenager comes to his parents with sincere feelings or honest opinions, which they explain away or tell him not to worry about and then they give him reasons why he should not feel as he does. When this occurs, verbal interaction is minimized and children will not communicate as frequently with their parents. A few examples emphasize this point.

Your thirteen-year-old daughter comes home and says that her boyfriend has broken up with her. She is devastated, her whole world has collapsed, she will never love anybody else for the rest of her life, she does not know how she is going to live without Glenn. . . . The typical parental response in this situation would be to try to "fix" the teenager's feelings—in other words, try to make her feel better. You might tell her, "You're a beautiful girl. This was the first boy that you have ever liked. There are many fish in the sea. You are certain to find another boyfriend. You're still so young." In other words, you are saying things to make her feel better; yet, in a sense, you are not really dealing with or trying to understand her feelings. You are trying to explain them away. Rather than doing this, the parent might give an example of a similar relationship that she/he had experienced and convey that the feeling is understood and that the parent knows how the child feels.

Another adolescent comes home from school and says, "My teacher is stupid. She really makes me mad. Look at all the homework she has given us. She must think that all we have to do is to stay inside and work." The typical parent response might be, "Let's see what she has given you." After seeing the assignments, the parent then responds, "That's not very much. She's only giving you this amount to help you learn. She's concerned about you and wants you to get a good job when you grow up." In other words, the parent is saying, "You shouldn't feel that way." A better response might be, "One time my boss gave me so much work to do that I felt I would never finish it. It really made me angry too. I thought he was the meanest person in the world. I understand how you feel."

The children in these examples are expressing genuine feelings, gut-level reactions. The first child is upset and unhappy and the second one is angry. The typical parent usually responds in a way that tends to negate or explain away the teenager's feelings. In situations like those in the examples, a parent does not have to agree or disagree with the child, but should try to understand and accept the adolescent's emotions and feelings. For example, if I tell you, "I'm scared to death that the building we are in is going to fall down and hurt us. I'm really afraid, nervous, and upset," what I do *not* want to hear you say is, "You shouldn't be afraid. This is a well-constructed building. It's not going to fall down. You don't have to worry. Anyway, buildings very seldom collapse." Maybe all you need to say is, "I was almost in an automobile accident one time and I was really scared and nervous. I know exactly how you feel." With this brief statement, you have accepted and understood my feelings. With teenagers, this assurance may be what is necessary. At times, you do not have to try to make them feel better, tell them they should not feel like that, explain away their feelings, or point out the inaccuracy or inappropriateness of their feelings. The communication from the child may involve his feelings, his attitudes, his perception of the situation, or an opinion. By responding to the child in a way that indicates that you understand how he feels, rather than by agreeing or disagreeing with his statements, the probability that he will keep talking will be increased. The teenager who feels that his parents understand his feelings will be more comfortable in relating to them and will talk with them more frequently.

Look for Underlying Feelings. This problem is a little more difficult than the others discussed in this Key and the previous one because it involves interpreting or reading into the adolescent's communications. Sometimes when children are talking to us, there may be emotions hidden behind what they say. But if we focus only on the behavior or the words, we may overlook their true feelings. Therefore, it is often necessary to look for the feelings behind the words or behaviors in order to respond effectively and maintain communication. Two examples follow.

Suppose a father had agreed to take his daughter out on Saturday for her first driving lesson. Naturally she is all excited and cannot wait until the weekend. When Saturday arrives, however, it is storming, and the forecast predicts an all-day rain. Nevertheless, she says to her father, "Let's go driving." He explains to her the reasons they cannot practice in the rain. However, his explanations do not satisfy her and she still persists, "Why can't we go in the rain? I'll be careful." The father then repeats the reasons and adds several more, but the teenager keeps insisting. Numerous explanations and a hundred whys later, the girl is still asking to go and is upset.

A boy comes storming into the house, slamming doors and saying, "Mr. Billings is a jerk! He's the stupidest person I know!" After listening to him rant and rave for a while, his Mom asks, "What's the matter?" The child goes on to explain that Mr. Billings agreed to pay him for cutting the grass, then after the job was done, did not pay him. When the youngster continues to carry on, the mother responds by telling him, "Stop acting like that. Control your temper. You had better not slam the door again. If you break it, you are going to have to pay for it."

The parents in these examples are focusing only on the adolescent's behavior or words and not on the feelings behind the action or communication. While there is a great deal of verbal activity, it is not effective communication and has satisfied no one.

One possible way to improve communication and satisfy the teenager is not to listen only to what she says or focus on the behavior, but to look behind the verbalizations and actions for the feelings being expressed. In both of the above situations, the children are frustrated, dissatisfied, disappointed, and angry. Rather than offering various explanations over and over again or focusing on the behavior displayed, the parent could respond to the underlying feelings. This approach is somewhat similar to the previous section, which discussed trying to understand the teenager's feelings.

With the young girl who was planning to take her first driving lesson, her father might have said, "We planned to go today, but it's raining and we can't go. You must be angry and disappointed. I remember when I was young and had saved money a long time to get my first car, but when I went to buy it, they didn't have the one I wanted in stock. I had to order it and wait six weeks for it. I was disappointed and annoyed. Is that how you feel?" As the child starts expressing her feelings, the father could focus on this rather than on the verbalizations. Then he could talk about driving the next day. In the example of the boy who was not paid for cutting grass for someone, the parent could have focused on the child's feelings rather than his behavior and have him sit down and talk about his anger and resentment. This approach would probably minimize the destructive behavior and his ranting and raving.

Reflecting the feelings behind what the teenager says is an effective method of communication and may often prevent negative interaction (getting upset with the child or scolding him) and provide the type of interaction he needs to satisfy him.

Nonverbal Communication. A number of books have been written on body language and nonverbal communication. Feelings, attitudes, interests, and disinterest can be communicated to others by things like tone of voice, body posture, and facial expressions. In other words, communication can occur without words. In dealing with the teenager, you should look for nonverbal cues that indicate some of the feelings the teenager is experiencing. For example, when talking to you, she may be showing some nervous habit or may become fidgety, indicating some tension or discomfort. This topic is similar in some ways to the section on looking for underlying feelings or looking beyond the child's verbalizations to identify underlying feelings.

You also must look at the way you are physically reacting to the teenager's communication. One time I was working with a sixteen-year-old who told me that his mother believed he was a liar most of the time and that she did not trust what he said. When I talked to the mother, she said this was not true and she could not recall ever telling her son that he was a liar. In a discussion with the teenager and his mother in my office, the child agreed that the mother did not actually call him a liar, but he added, "She gives me those eyes. When she rolls her eyes, I know she doesn't believe me." The mother said that she did not believe this happens and thought the child was just overreacting and being oversensitive. As the discussion progressed, we began talking about other topics, such as the boy's chores and responsibilities around the house. Many times when the mother did not agree with the boy or thought he was not telling the whole truth, she would roll her eyes and look at him in a particular way. After several instances of this, the boy commented, "See what I mean? See what she's doing with her eyes?" When the mother became aware of this behavior, she agreed that this happened frequently when she felt that she was not getting the whole truth or that something was being exaggerated. Once she realized her reaction and its impact on her son, she was then able to change it.

You do not have to directly tell a child that you are aggravated with what she is saying or disinterested in the conversation. This information can be conveyed by your facial expression, your body posture, the way you look at the child, and other nonverbal factors. This type of communication will reduce the amount of interaction your teenager will have with you.

It Is Not What They Say But How They Say It. The old saying "Children should be seen and not heard" certainly does not promote communication between parent and child. We want the adolescent to communicate with us. Because teenagers are developing opinions and attitudes that may differ from ours, disagreements and differences of opinion will become part of the communication. You want to hear things that your teenager is displeased with in the family environment, what he would like changed, how he would like to be treated. Parents should welcome expression of these feelings and others that are not consistent with ours. However, it is not so much what the teenager says, but the manner and tone in which he says it.

Frequently, when I am talking with a child, she will say, "My parents don't understand me. They never listen to anything I say. They never consider my feelings." After more discussion, the child gives me an example of what she means. Perhaps she has asked her father for permission to go to a concert with her friends and he has refused. I then ask the child, "What did you say?" In a calm, adult manner, the child starts telling me exactly what she said. After she has finished, I remark, "That makes a lot of sense to me. I can understand where you're coming from, but did you talk to your father in the same manner that you are talking to me?" After reflection, the usual response is "No." The teen did not communicate this information in a calm way and instead used a flippant, argumentative, or sarcastic manner and then began screaming, mumbling, or complaining while telling the parent how she felt about the decision.

Many teenagers only express their feelings and dislikes to their parents when they are upset. This usually results in a shouting match. I often tell the adolescent, "When people holler and scream at me, I really do not hear what they say. All I hear is the hollering and screaming. When people attack, I tend to attack back. And if you're the child and I'm the adult, guess who gets into the most trouble?"

When the preceding situation is common in a family with adolescents, the teenagers start communication with their parents about things they do not like and things they would like changed. However, this should not be done during an argument, but at other times when no one is upset and the youngsters have a chance to talk calmly with the parents. At the same time, I inform the parents that I have asked their child to start communicating her feelings about what is going on at home that the youngster does not like and would like to have changed. However, I have also told the child that I want her to express her feelings calmly in an adult manner. No hollering, fresh talk, or flippant attitude. If the child is communicating her feelings in this fashion, the parent should listen, try to understand the feelings, and make changes when possible. In addition, if you can get the child to express some of her dislikes, you have tools to use in a compromise. For instance, if a child is able to express to you that he is dissatisfied with the curfew you have set, you might be able to use this situation as a compromise: If he improves on his schoolwork, you will allow him to stay out later.

Adolescence is a period of rebellion and of striving for independence; consequently there will be many areas where children will disagree with you or not see things exactly the way you do. Remember, *what* they say is not as important as *how* they say it. If they communicate their disapprovals and disagreements with family policies and the way they are treated, certainly listen to them and when possible try to respond positively. The child who says to his parent, "I think I should be able to spend more time on the phone. Fifteen minutes a day is not enough. I've been doing all my homework and my grades are good," should be responded to in a very different manner from the child who begins by ranting and raving about his lack of phone time.

It should be acceptable for a teenager to tell his mother that he does not like eating liver on Monday nights. However, it would be totally unacceptable for him to come into the kitchen on Monday evening and start threatening his mother that he will not eat this "garbage" and that she had better learn to cook something "decent."

In trying to show the adolescent how to express his feelings of disapproval in an appropriate fashion, I often use the following example. Let's say I ask your opinion of my shirt. Suppose you really do not like it and think it looks terrible. Now, you could respond to me in several different ways. You could tell me, "That shirt looks like garbage. I wouldn't even use it to wash my car." Or you could say, "You must have been drunk when you bought that shirt. Nobody in his right mind would buy something like that." Or you could just say, "I don't care for that shirt." The same thing has been expressed in three different ways. In the first two ways, I am going to read what you're saying as an attack, and will probably attack back and not understand what you are saying. In the third expression of your feelings, I heard exactly what you said and now I have a better chance to respond appropriately.

We should encourage the child to express his feelings and opinions to us, but we want him to do so in an appropriate, calm, and adultlike manner. Therefore, this communication should not occur in the heat of an argument or when things are not going his way. Try to discuss areas of discontent at times other than during a conflict. This advice holds true for the parent as well as the teenager.

20

COMMUNICATION: THINGS TO REMEMBER

1. Remember that during adolescence communication generally decreases and that a child will confide less in parents. This is a fairly normal process and should not be overreacted to.

2. Listen to what is being said; that is, try to understand the teenager's feelings and where she is coming from. Rather than thinking about arguments or retaliations, listen to her.

3. Stop what you are doing and look at the teenager. Listen when she speaks to you. Be sure that you are giving her the proper attention and that she is not talking to a newspaper or to your back.

4. Be sure most of your communication is positive, not negative. Don't dwell on mistakes, failures, misbehaviors, or something they forgot to do. Give them positive communication and talk about their successes, accomplishments, interests, and appropriate behavior.

5. Talk to them about their interests (e.g., music, sports, computers, dance-team practice, cars, motorcycles). Have conversations with them when you are not trying to make a point, to teach them something, or to impress them. Talk to them just to talk and to have positive verbal interaction.

6. Avoid talking too much—giving long or too-detailed explanations, repeating lectures, questioning excessively, or using other forms of communication that will result in the teenager turning a deaf ear to you.

7. Try to understand the teen's feelings. You do not have to agree or disagree with him, just make him aware that you understand how he feels. Do not try to explain away his emotions. There are times that you do not have to fix things or make the youngster feel better. Understanding how he feels may be the primary comfort that is needed.

8. Do not overreact to what is said. Remember, sometimes teenagers say things that are designed to get a reaction from their parents. In addition, do not say no too fast. Sometimes it is better to think about the request and give a response later. In other words, think before you open your mouth.

9. Try to create situations in which communication can occur (driving the child to the doctor's appointment, having the teenager help you with household tasks). You have to be physically close to the teenager for communication to occur. A television in the adolescent's room can be an additional barrier to family communication. Whenever possible, the parent should try to do things *with* the teenager, rather than separately. Although the child may not frequently accept them, provide opportunities for him to do things with you.

10. Try to avoid power struggles, confrontation, and arguing matches. Your goal should be to have the communication move toward a compromise situation rather than a battle. When appropriate, involve the teenager in decision-making and setting consequences for his or her behavior.

21

~~~~~~

ANGER AND REBELLIOUS BEHAVIOR

No matter what we do, a certain amount of anger, opposition, stubbornness, and resistance will be present in the teenager. During this period of the child's life, our major goal is to avoid compounding or increasing this amount. Certain ways of dealing with the teenager will intensify these feelings; others will not. This Key will discuss effective and ineffective techniques of dealing with these typical teenage emotions and behaviors.

In general, anger is a form of disapproval. If you are angry with me, it means that I am saying or doing something that you do not like. Similarly, if your teenager is showing aggressive or rebellious behavior toward you, his peers, or authority figures, it means that he disapproves of or does not agree with what you or someone else is saying or doing.

Ways of Expressing Anger. Disapproval, anger, and rebellious behaviors can be expressed in a variety of ways. Some are effective and appropriate, while others are ineffective and result in more problems than they solve. Suppose a teenager is going to a school dance and asks his parents if after the dance he can go out with his friends to eat. The parents say no and tell him to come home right after the dance.

The child asks several times if this request can be granted, but the answer remains no. This teenager can handle his feelings of frustration and anger in five basic ways:

1. *He can express his feelings in an appropriate manner.* In other words, he can discuss the feelings with his parents in a calm, adult manner. ("I really don't like you treating me like a baby and making me come home right after the dance. All of my friends are going to be there and I'm going to look stupid if I have to come home right after the dance and can't go out to eat. It makes me angry when you treat me that way. I really don't ask for too much, but every time I want a favor or some more privileges, now that I'm older, the answer is still always no.")

2. *He can keep these feelings and emotions to himself,* comply with what the parents say, and say nothing.

3. *He can express his disapproval indirectly through a variety of passive-aggressive maneuvers* (stubbornness, opposition, complaining under his breath, doing just the opposite of what he's told, going out to eat anyway, leaving a mess in the kitchen).

4. *He can express his anger directly through verbal or physical actions* (screaming and hollering, name-calling, cursing, or attempting to hit the person whom he perceives as the source of his anger).

5. *He can displace his feelings to a less threatening person or to an inanimate object.* (Although the teenager is angry with his mother, he may hit his sister, throw something, slam a door, or punch a wall.)

As you can see, some ways of dealing with aggressive feelings, anger, and disapproval of others are inappropriate and will get the teenager in trouble, while others will not. Following is a more detailed discussion of these five basic ways.

Appropriate Expression of Feelings. The teenager who is upset or angry with someone can express his feelings in an appropriate adultlike manner. He does not need to yell or become sarcastic or flippant. He can simply communicate his feelings to the other person. For example, if an adolescent feels as though his father is always on his back, criticizing him and pointing out everything he does wrong, he might say, "I don't like you yelling at me every time I do something wrong. It makes me feel bad and hurts my feelings. It seems as if you never say anything when I do something right or what I'm supposed to do. You only point out when I'm doing something wrong." In this situation, the teenager is expressing his feelings and is not being fresh if he uses a normal conversational tone.

We should strive to have our child communicate his feelings of disapproval, resentment, and anger. If children can express their anger without shouting or being fresh, rude, or smart, we should reinforce the communication and listen to them. Some parents view an appropriate expression of feelings as disrespect or impertinence, but this is a mistake.

The teenager is forming opinions and attitudes that may be different from ours. We should want to hear what he disapproves of, what makes him happy, and what makes him angry. This appropriate way to express anger will produce few, if any, problems in parent-teenager interaction. The more the adolescent is able to communicate his likes and dislikes to you, the more opportunity you have to understand him and arrive at compromises.

Suppression of Feelings. This is simply the bottling up of emotions. When some teenagers become angry or disapprove of something, they do not say anything, but keep their feelings to themselves. Consequently, others are not aware of how these youngsters really feel. This usually results in frustration on the part of the teen and the buildup of further anger.

These feelings of disapproval or resentment will eventually emerge in one form or another. A teenager who does not express her emotions and bottles them up instead of saying how she feels may express these feelings by other means, such as headaches or depression. Teenagers who deal with their aggressive feelings in this manner are often more of a problem to themselves than to others. However, this type of child may explode when faced with very minor frustrations or disappointments. Some small event occurs and all the anger and resentment that have been suppressed erupt. A seemingly insignificant event becomes the "straw that breaks the camel's back."

Passive-Aggressive Methods. The passive-aggressive techniques are the ones most frequently used by teenagers. These are indirect or passive ways of expressing anger, such as stubbornness, opposition, resistance, complaining under the breath, saying or doing things to get a reaction from you, contradicting you, forgetting to do things, putting off chores. They may look at you as if you are crazy when you try to give them a lecture.

Suppose your boss really gives you a hard time the first thing one morning at work. He tells you what a bad job you are doing, yells at you, and says that because of your ineffective performance you may be fired. You become extremely angry and upset with him, but you cannot punch him in the nose because you will be fired. You cannot quit the job because you need it. What can you do? You slow down your work pace and do a little less. Or you take a longer coffee break or lunch hour or forget to do a few things he told you to do. What has happened is that you have passively acknowledged your anger in an attempt to express your feelings.

Teenagers frequently use this indirect method to express their anger. Often, it takes the form of rebellion, doing the opposite of what is desired, negativism, doing something annoying, having the last word. For example, you tell your son to cut the grass before he leaves the house, and he forgets. You're getting ready to go out to eat and you tell your daughter to wear some nice clothes, but instead she puts on a faded pair of jeans and a holey T-shirt. When you are out shopping with your teen and you say that you like a particular outfit, she responds emphatically that she hates it. When you tell your son to collect the garbage and put it out, he does the job but not without mumbling under his breath the whole time—you know he is saying something nasty about you, but you cannot understand it. The stereo is booming, but when you tell your child to turn down the volume, instead she turns it up.

When teenagers use this method of dealing with aggressive and angry feelings, it is likely to produce problems in relationships with others, especially those in a position of supervision or direction over them (e.g., parents, teachers).

Acting Out. This method involves directly acting out feelings of anger or disapproval. This may involve verbal or physical aggression. The teenager who is angry may strike out at the parents in a verbal manner by talking back, hollering, or cursing. Acting out can also involve physical violence such as fighting or hitting. The adolescent directly retaliates—either verbally or physically—against the source of his or her anger. This method of dealing with aggressive feelings will certainly produce problems in peer interaction and also in relationships with authority.

111

Displacing Feelings. When teenagers become angry, they sometimes do not deal directly with the source of their feelings or express them appropriately. Instead, they displace these emotions by transferring them to a less threatening person or an inanimate object. For example, your employer gives you some trouble at work and you are angry at her. You come home and shout at your wife. Your wife then yells at the kids. The kids kick the dog. The dog chases the cat. These feelings are being directed to another source. Some other examples: A mother and a son get into a confrontation, and the teenager becomes very angry with his mother. However, he does not say or do anything to his parent, but a few minutes later goes into his brother's room and starts a fight. A teacher reprimands a teenager and when the girl comes home from school, she starts giving her mother a hard time. A child who has been grounded for talking back storms off to his room, slamming doors, and kicking his furniture.

22

~~~~~~

TECHNIQUES TO AVOID THE BUILDUP OF ANGER

As discussed in Key 21, all teenagers occasionally grow angry and rebellious and express these emotions in some fashion. Some methods of acknowledging aggressive feelings produce problems, others don't.

Anger and feelings of disapproval build up and then are released through different methods. We can exemplify this situation by using the image of an "anger" balloon. Each time something happens that we do not like, air is forced into the balloon and it starts to expand. Eventually, air has to be let out of the balloon. How anger is expressed is different for different people. Some people let anger build up until their balloon pops, and when this happens there may be an explosive outburst of anger over a minor annoyance. After this display of anger, there is usually a period of control until the balloon blows up again. Other people release air from the balloon every time it starts to fill. These are the individuals who appropriately express their feelings at the time they occur. Some other individuals release air through passive-aggressive maneuvers, displacement, or physical complaints.

In addition to helping the teenager appropriately express and deal with his or her angry feelings, parents should try to reduce the accumulation of anger and deal appropriately with aggressive and rebellious behaviors when they occur. The techniques that follow should help.

Encourage Appropriate Communication. The most effective way to deal with anger and rebellious behavior is to have teenagers appropriately communicate their feelings of disapproval and resentment. Encourage them to express and explain negative feelings, sources of anger, and their opinions—that is, what angers them, what we do that they do not like, what they disapprove of. If a teenager expresses emotions appropriately, in a normal tone of voice, she should not be viewed as rude or disrespectful. This is an appropriate expression of anger, and the youngster should not be reprimanded or punished. In other words, allow teenagers to complain, disagree, or disapprove provided they are not sarcastic, flippant, or nasty. Remember, though, that allowing a child to shout, swear, or be fresh does not teach effective communication of emotions.

Listen. If the teenager is complaining about excessive restrictions, punishments, or other things that she does not like, *listen.* Try to understand her feelings. If the complaints are realistic, see if something can be worked out and resolved or if a compromise can be achieved. See Keys 18 and 19 for some additional advice in this area.

Avoid Excessive Negative Attention. It's a mistake to pay more attention to what the child is doing wrong—his failures, mistakes, misbehaviors—than to what he is doing right—his successes, achievements, good behaviors. When you go to bed at night, review the day you have had with your child. Have you spent as much time during the day looking at his appropriate behaviors as you have looking at his inappropriate actions? You should avoid using punishment as a primary method of control. Instead, substitute positive consequences, which place the emphasis on good behavior rather than on bad behavior. Eliminate verbal punishment (hollering, putting down the adolescent, name-calling, excessive criticism), and use reward as a disciplinary tactic. (See Keys 11 and 12 for more information.) Emphasize successes, accomplishments, achievements, and good behaviors. Pay more attention to normal good behavior and be positive.

Constant nagging of a teenager will certainly result in a buildup of anger, resentment, and aggressive behaviors. See Key 15 for more information in this area.

Try Not to React to Passive-Aggressive Behavior. Some of the opposition, stubbornness, resistance, and other passive-aggressive maneuvers of teenagers are designed to express anger and/or to get reaction from the parents. Ignoring is often an effective way to reduce this behavior.

Some ways of dealing with this passive-aggressive behavior will result in the development of more anger, while others will help deflate the anger balloon. For example, a child is told to set the table for dinner. While setting the table, she mumbles under her breath and every now and then you hear comments like, "They think I'm a slave. I want to go live at Grandma's, where I'm appreciated." Along with the mumbling, she is angrily tossing ice in the glasses and banging down the plates and silverware. This teenager is annoyed because she feels she has better things to do than set the table. Her mumbling and other actions are passive-aggressive maneuvers to express her anger and resentment. These behaviors are releasing anger and letting air out of the anger balloon. If you react to her mumbling by criticizing or scolding, you will be putting more air back into the balloon—that is, the anger that was initially released by the child's complaining and defiance will be offset by a buildup of additional aggressive feelings. By using the consequence of ignoring, this additional buildup of anger can be eliminated.

There are several things that must be kept in mind when using this consequence and there are a few different ways to ignore. (See Keys 16 and 17 for more information on this area.) In general, if you ask a teenager to do something and he is doing it, although complaining the whole time, ignore his complaints since he is doing what you asked.

Avoid Random Discipline. Parents often discipline after the fact. I call this random discipline. They set a rule and wait for the adolescent to break it before they decide upon a consequence. To teenagers, the concept of fairness is extremely important and if disciplined in this fashion, they may frequently feel unjustly treated. In addition, random discipline often makes teenagers feel that others are responsible for what has happened to them and anger is apt to develop. You should spell out the rules and consequences for your child's behavior at the same time. The most important part of this process is not the rule but the consequence. Put the responsibility for what happens to the child squarely on his or her shoulders. See Key 7 for more techniques on how to avoid the buildup of anger caused by random disciplining.

Don't Get Into a Power Struggle. You tell the adolescent to clean his room and he refuses. Then you threaten, "You had better clean it or you're not going out on Saturday." He replies, "You can't make me clean it and I'm going out on Saturday anyway." Then you say something, he says something, you both begin to shout, and a full-blown power struggle has developed. This is a good way to generate anger in your child.

When possible, avoid battles and power struggles, which only lead to a buildup of anger. At times, it may be better to have the child experience the consequence of his behavior rather than to win the battle and get him to do what you want. If you try to win each fight, you battle the child throughout adolescence and will probably end up losing the war. This concept is discussed in detail in Key 6.

Look for Ways to Compromise. In many situations with adolescents, you should try to treat them the way you would one of your friends or another adult. Rather than get into a battle to see who is going to win, it may be better to create a situation where a compromise is reached. See Key 6 for a fuller discussion of this topic.

Provide Appropriate Models. Children learn a great deal from modeling their parents' behavior. The way we handle our conflicts and problems is apt to be imitated by our children. If I handle my anger by hollering, throwing things, or hitting, there is a good possibility that my children will handle their conflicts in a similar fashion. The old saying "Don't do as I do, do as I say" is a very ineffective way of dealing with behavior. Therefore, if you see aggressive or rebellious behaviors in your teenager, look at yourself, your spouse, or an older sibling to see if one of you is modeling these behaviors. If so, the behavior must stop before we can expect to change the adolescent's conduct

If there is a significant amount of arguing in the home or if parents demonstrate disrespect for one another, it is likely the teenager will adapt similar behavior patterns. If you scream at your child, he is likely to scream back.

One mother told me, "Every time I hit my daughter, she hits me back. What should I do?" My answer was very simple: "Stop hitting her." Whenever I see a child who is showing aggressive-type behaviors, I want to know if this behavior is being modeled in the home. If youngsters are dealt with through physical punishment, we may be teaching them to handle conflicts by physical force or aggressive behavior. It

117

does not have to be the actual use of physical force. It can be threats of force. In other words, "I'm going to get you to do that because I am bigger than you and can control you by intimidation." If we deal with teenagers in that fashion, we are apt to cause a buildup of anger at the same time that we are indirectly teaching them aggressive and inappropriate methods of problem solving.

Parents who use physical punishment with the young child as a primary method of dealing with his or her behavior forget one important thing: children grow and usually get as big as or bigger than them. A young child disciplined through physical punishment will probably end up an adolescent who gets into physical battles with his parents.

Parents must look at themselves to be sure they are not models of the behavior they are trying to eliminate in the child. Serving as an appropriate model is a good way to teach children how to deal with and express anger.

Who's in Control? When I was a young parent, people would tell me, "Little kids, little problems. Big kids, big problems." At the time, I did not quite understand this bit of advice, but now that I have experienced being the parent of teenagers, I know exactly what it means.

Young children who have been pampered and spoiled and have learned how to control their parents are used to having things their own way. Therefore, they tend to be somewhat bossy and self-centered, behaviors that intensify during adolescence. If a child like this is told not to eat any cookies, he may defy the parents, sneak into the kitchen, and eat the cookies. Or if he is told not to jump on the couch, he does not listen and continues jumping. When adolescence arrives, the same child is told to be home by midnight and instead comes home at 4:00 A.M. Told not to drink and drive, he drinks and drives anyway. The little problems of the small child become much bigger during adolescence and frequently result in more serious consequences.

I often see families where adolescents are out of control, will not take no for an answer, and will not accept parental authority. Many times when these teens do not get their way, aggressive, rebellious, and oppositional behavior results. Some of these adolescents have been in control of the family since they were young. The child determined the routines and activities in the home more than the parents. A seven-year-old was having trouble in school because she was not doing the required work in class, but instead was day-dreaming and doing whatever she pleased. In talking with the parents, I discovered that they were having the same type of difficulty at home. The child would not cooperate, especially with routine tasks. They also mentioned that she was constantly complaining to them about the fact that her three- and four-year-old brothers did not have to go to school. Why did she have to? She did not think it was fair that her brothers could stay home, play, and watch television. Every morning before school, an argument about this usually took place. She frequently requested to stay home, and generally this issue produced a great deal of conflict in the home. In order to solve the situation, the parents put the two brothers in nursery school, demonstrating that the daughter was more in control than the parents. Rather than allow a child to call the shots and try to manipulate the environment to accommodate the child or to avoid problems, it might be better to have the child learn that there are certain things that must be done whether or not she wants to do them.

As I mentioned earlier, we can control young children, but with the adolescent we must exert authority. I am not talking about an authority by force or by dictatorship. I am

119

talking about an authority that involves setting rules and being consistent in administering consequences. If parents can exert this type of authority, the probability that positive behaviors and attitudes can be developed will increase.

The child who has been in control his entire life finds it difficult to relinquish this power during adolescence. However, because of the severity of the consequences that can occur in adolescence, parents are usually trying to exert more control at this time. As a result, battles, conflicts, anger, and resentment occur when the teenager does not have his own way. Key 7 and Key 23 offer some techniques on establishing rules and consequences in a fashion that will allow you to have some authority over the teenager.

Stabilize the Environment. Teenagers who experience environmental change—especially divorce, separation, or remarriage—may develop underlying anger. The anger and resentment that result from the changes may be expressed in other ways. Try to identify the changes, stabilize the environment, and get him to express his feelings through more appropriate methods. If the adolescent has questions regarding a divorce or remarriage, discuss them with him.

Avoid Excessive Restrictions. Some children who are overprotected, excessively restricted, and generally not allowed to be like other youngsters their age may develop resentment and anger. They want to do things that others do, but are prevented from doing so. Sometimes you have to look at your teenager's peer group in order to decide what is and is not appropriate and what is too much restriction.

Do Not Let the Behavior Get Out of Control. Once a child is actively involved in an aggressive behavior or shouting match, it is difficult to deal with the behavior. Rather than wait till the behavior occurs to handle it, sometimes it is possible, and better, to try to prevent it from happening or to catch it early and not let it get out of control. In some teenagers, the aggressive behavior develops gradually and may involve several steps. Some initial behaviors appear and then intensify. For example, a teenager's brother may call him stupid. Some verbal exchanges follow, then a pushing and shoving match begins, and finally a full-blown fight erupts. Rather than wait to react when the fight starts, it would be better to try to catch the behavior early and intervene before the situation gets out of hand. Target the name-calling or verbal arguing and try to stop that, rather than wait to zero in on the fighting.

A mother tells her sixteen-year-old son to clean his room. When he says no, she counters back with a warning, then a threat. A struggle develops, and after some shouting and screaming on both parts, the boy goes to his room and throws something, breaking the window. Rather than waiting to zero in on the boy's destructive behavior, it would be better for the parent to catch this sequence in the beginning.

23

^^

TRUST AND RESPONSIBLE BEHAVIORS

Some of the typical complaints of the adolescent are:

- They treat me like a child and won't let me do anything everybody my age does.
- They have to know everything I do and every place I go.
- I need more freedom. They restrict me too much.
- I'm old enough to drive the car, but they won't let me.
- They're always on my case about schoolwork and homework. I'm old enough to know what I have to do.
- I don't see why I have to have a time limit when I talk on the phone.

In general, these statements indicate a teenager feels his parents are restrictive, treat him like a child, and don't grant him privileges other kids his age have. A main reason parents will not let teenagers do what they want is that the parents do not feel they can trust the youngsters to be responsible enough to handle the loosening of restrictions. Many parents describe teenagers as lacking self-discipline or internal controls and failing to do what they are supposed to.

Parents complain:

- Whenever he doesn't get his way, he flies off of the handle, gets upset, and acts like a five-year-old. I can't allow him to get behind the wheel of a car. What do you think would happen if he got angry while he was driving?
- I can't trust her. She tells me one thing and then does something else.
- He's fourteen years old, but I still have to tell him to brush his teeth and often have to check that he does it. How can I treat him like a grownup?
- She never cleans her room. I have to force her to do routine duties. How many times do I have to tell her to do these things before she'll just do them without being told?

Parents lose trust in their children when the children say one thing and then do something different. To "How are you doing in school?" Susie may answer, "Fine," but when the report card comes, she has failed three subjects. Or Jason may report, "I'm going to Clark's house," yet when you call Clark's house, his mother says that your son has not been there. On Friday afternoon as they leave the house, your teenagers may say, "We're going to a movie," but they go someplace else.

A lack of trust develops when a teenager lies, steals, is irresponsible, or is manipulative. The adolescent shows a lack of responsibility or self-discipline when he does not do what he is supposed to do. You cannot always believe what he says, you may have difficulty depending on him to do things, he is often forgetful, or he may frequently lose his belongings. A teenager may be pleasure-oriented and want to do his own thing, take the easiest way out, and do just enough to get by. Some children see no reason to do the unpleasant. If you ask them to do something they want to do, they will give you 100 percent of their effort. However, if you ask them to do something they do not want to do—no matter how easy or small—it will never get done. They often have difficulty following daily household routines or classroom procedures. You have to constantly remind them or force them to do what is expected. They lack responsibility.

In order for parents to develop trust, the teenager must exhibit responsible behaviors. A child who shows responsible behaviors generally gets more freedom and privileges.

There seem to be several ways that children acquire responsible behavior.

Genetic. Some children seem to be born to responsibility, as if they acquired it through heredity. They display this behavior from an early age, and it continues throughout their lives. They are generally cooperative teenagers, who do as they're told and even do some things before being told. They keep their rooms neat, do their homework and class preparation, put away clothes, help with chores around the house. It is easy to develop trust in these children.

"Attitude Kids." You can develop responsible behaviors in some children by talking to them and establishing or changing an attitude. It seems as if these youngsters develop an attitude first and then acquire the desired behavior. An attitude can be established by giving children information, explaining things to them, reasoning, being logical, or getting them to see the situation from a different angle. We may tell the teenager, "If you wash your face several times a day, that will minimize acne and you will not have to go to the dermatologist as often" or "If you take care of your clothes and hang them up instead of throwing them on the floor, they will last longer and look nicer." After hearing these reasons a few times, the adolescent complies with the request. I call children like this "attitude kids."

For these children, it's as if a lightbulb comes on and the behavior follows. After you explain the importance of homework and a good education, the "attitude kid" then behaves accordingly and does well in school. Reasoning, explaining, lectures, and the like work exceptionally well. It is enough to warn, "Don't touch the pot on the stove. It's hot, and you'll get burned." Responsible behaviors are developed fairly easily in these children and it is easy to trust them.

"Behavior Kids." For some children the behavior has to be established *first* and then the attitude follows. Some children can be told many times to clean their room, but will still leave it messy. Their parents could explain the cost of living, inflation, or the number of hours they had to work to buy the clothes, but the jacket, pants, and shirts would still end up on the floor. These teenagers do not develop responsible attitudes from discussions with parents. Parents must first establish the behavior (i.e., get them into the habit of doing something), and then the attitude will follow. Talking, reasoning, excessive explaining, lectures, shouting, screaming, or other verbal interaction does not work with these adolescents. They develop attitudes and responsible behaviors only by experiencing consequences. I call youngsters like these "behavior kids."

With the "attitude kid," a lightbulb comes on first (i.e., the attitude is established) and then the behavior follows. With the "behavior kid," the lightbulb comes on but it is very, very dim and increases in intensity each time we are able to get him to perform the behavior. In other words, the attitude develops gradually over time as he repeats the behavior. The more we can get him to behave in a certain way, and something happens that he likes or does not like, the faster the attitude develops. This child has to experience the consequences of his behavior. He has to touch the pot to learn that hot pots will cause him pain. It may be fine to explain why a child needs to do homework or clean his room, but the most important thing with the "behavior kid" is what is going to happen to him if he performs and what is going to happen to him if he does not perform. After explaining the importance of an education and the need to do homework, the parent might tell this child, "You've been giving me a hassle every night about doing your homework. You either don't do it, complain, or do it halfway. From now on, every night that you do all the homework and cooperate and are pleasant, you will be able to play a video game that night. If you give me trouble, you will not be allowed to."

This type of teenager does not come to us with a lot of self-discipline, internal control, or responsibility, and it is somewhat difficult to trust him. He needs external controls and structure to help him develop internal control. The more this teenager is on his own—in an unstructured setting where he must rely on his internal control, in a situation where the consequences of his behavior are the same (he gets to play a video game whether he does or does not cooperate with homework), or in a situation where there is a general lack of limits on his behavior—the more he will manifest irresponsible behaviors.

24

‸‸‸

TECHNIQUES TO DEVELOP TRUST AND RESPONSIBLE BEHAVIORS

Many teenagers who have trouble with trust and responsibility are similar to the "behavior kids"; in order to develop self-discipline and a responsible attitude, they must first develop the desired behavior (cleaning their room, doing their homework, coming home on time). In other words, the focus is more on behavior than on attitude. After the behavior is developed, hopefully an appropriate attitude will gradually be established. The following techniques help the child develop self-discipline, responsibility, and trust.

Define the Rule and the Consequence. You must tell the teenager what you expect, but more important than the rule is what will happen if she complies with your request and what will happen if she does not. Spell out rules and consequences at the same time. Put the responsibility onto the adolescent's shoulders. If good things happen to her, it is up to her. If bad things happen, it is also up to her.

The general techniques of setting rules and consequences are discussed in detail in Key 10. I would suggest that you review this Key, because these rules are the primary techniques that are used to develop responsible behaviors.

When trying to develop responsibility in youngsters, many parents focus primarily on assigning chores (cutting grass, putting out the garbage, feeding the dog). This is fine, but it is not the main way that children develop responsible behavior. Chores usually involve consequences; that is, if a child does not put out the garbage, he does not get his allowance. The reason that chores are often used to develop responsibility is that predictable consequences usually follow the teenager's behavior. Therefore, when you are trying to develop responsibility or self-discipline in your child, you should spell out the rule and the consequence before the rule is broken. Then whatever happens to the teenager is a result of his behavior and no one else's. Responsible behavior can be encouraged throughout the day with this method

Also, by spelling out consequences ahead of time, you avoid using random discipline and giving the teenager the impression that others are responsible for the consequence that has happened to him. This is extremely important to the adolescent, because with random discipline he feels unfairly treated. Most parents are careful and specific rule setters: "I want you home at 1:00 A.M., no later." However, many parents make the mistake of deciding the consequence *after* the teenager breaks the rule. Under these circumstances, the youngster is apt to feel unjustly treated. If an adolescent is dealt with primarily in this fashion, it is somewhat difficult for him to feel in control of what happens to him and to develop responsibility for his own behavior.

Tie All Consequences to the Child's Behavior. At first when trying to develop responsibility in some teenagers, it is best to tie as many consequences as possible to their behavior. In other words, you set up a situation where the adolescents will earn their rewards and pleasures, as well as their punishments and disappointments. Not only do you spell out disciplinary measures ahead of time, but you try to relate all consequences to their behavior. Put them in control of the consequences of their actions—good or bad.

- Tell the teenager who has been using the phone every night for doing nothing that she now has to earn this privilege by performing some chore.
- Set up a rule and a consequence for your son so that he no longer gets to use the car on weekends unless he shows you certain behaviors.
- Inform your daughter, who used to get on the Internet just for breathing, that she now has to perform certain duties in order to have access to the computer.

Avoid Assuming Responsibility. You should not assume responsibility for the teenager or her behavior. Make her responsible. If you force her to do her homework every night or do it for her, you are more responsible for the work being completed than the child. If you have to tell your son forty-seven times to take out the garbage before he complies, you are more responsible for the task than the child is. And the next night you will probably have to do the same thing. The teenager completes the task, but he doesn't develop responsibility or independent behavior. You may have to act as his motivator until he gets married or leaves the house.

For days a parent tells her child to clean his room, but it never gets done. Eventually, she gets fed up, drags him to the room, stands over him, and makes him clean it. In several minutes the room is spotless, but who is responsible for the room being cleaned? The parent. A better way to get this room cleaned and encourage responsibility in the teenager would be to spell out expectations and consequences ahead of time. Put the responsibility on the adolescent Avoid forcing him to do what he is supposed to do.

These same situations occur when parents allow a teenager to become dependent on them. Either the parents help the teenager excessively or else they do things for her. This may involve picking up after teens, keeping their rooms cleaned, waking them up for school, locating their keys. When parents act in this way, the adolescent finds it difficult to learn independent and responsible behaviors because it is easier to let someone else do things for her. Avoid allowing the teenager to become too dependent on you for performing tasks for her that she is physically capable of doing.

Children who are spoiled and often have their needs met for them, who are in more control than their parents, or who frequently get their own way also have a difficult time developing responsible behaviors. The same situation exists when parents "run interference" for the teenager and protect him from experiencing the consequences of his actions. This parent-child interaction should be avoided to establish self-discipline and responsibility.

Make the Consequences Different for Positive and for Negative Behaviors. Some teenagers do not develop responsible behaviors because the same thing happens to them whether they perform the required task or not. The adolescent thinks, "I'll be able to go out Friday night whether or not I cooperate around the house" or "I'll be able to use the computer whether or not I do my homework." If someone said to me, "You can go to work and I will pay you or you can stay home and I will pay you," I certainly would be out fishing instead of working. In fact, I would have to be stupid to go to work. The same situation exists for children who feel that if they get into a jam, they will be able to manipulate their way out of the situation and again they will not experience the consequences. You have to make the consequences different for teenagers if you expect to change their behavior or develop an attitude of responsibility. In other words, one thing will happen if the adolescent cooperates around the house, and something entirely different will happen if he does not cooperate. Be sure the teenager is experiencing different consequences for different behaviors.

Win the War and Forget About the Battles. Sometimes it is better to lose a few battles, but win the war. It may be more important for your teenager to experience the consequences of his behavior than it would be for you to get the task accomplished. For example, you say, "You cannot leave the house today until you clean the fish tank." He comes back with, "I don't care. I didn't want to go anywhere. I'm going in the den to watch television." Now you think, "What am I going to do now?" The answer is "Nothing." The rule sticks. In this example, getting the fish tank cleaned should be actually the fourth thing you are trying to accomplish. The first thing is to make the teenager aware that there will be two different consequences to his behavior, positive and negative. The second thing you are trying to achieve is to teach the child that he is responsible for his behavior. In other words, "Whether you go out in two minutes, two hours, two days, or two weeks, there is only one person in the entire world who can determine that and that is you. You are responsible for what happens to you." The third thing is to teach him: "I am going to do what you tell me to do. I am going to consistently follow through with the consequences that you decide. The consequences that happen to you depend totally on your actions. If you do not clean the fish tank, you are telling me that you do not want to leave the house and I am going to be sure that this happens. If you clean the tank, you are telling me that you want to go outside and I will follow through with that."

Sometimes, parents continually battle with a teenager—about homework, cleaning up the bathroom, picking up clothes, cleaning up after herself. They try to win each battle by forcing the child to do what they request. Although they eventually win each battle, the teenager does not develop any independent or responsible behavior. Your daughter refuses to help in the kitchen and you tell her, "If you do not help me, I will not be able to pick up your boyfriend after school tomorrow and bring him to the house. If you help me, I will be able to bring him." Now perhaps the child will refuse to help you in the kitchen and not have you pick up her boyfriend. You may look at this as, "I lost. She won." However, it is more important that she experience the consequences of not cooperating than that you force her to help. After this happens a few times, she may be more responsive when you say, "Would you please help me in the kitchen?" For some behaviors, it may not be important to get the child to comply. When the teenager experiences the consequences of her behavior today, you may get more cooperation tomorrow. Most times you can forget about the battles and focus on the war.

Do not get into power struggles if the teenager refuses to cooperate. You are dealing with a young adult and must exert a different form of control than used with the younger child. A parent tells a teenager to do something, he refuses, then an argument starts and develops into a power struggle. Avoid this scenario whenever possible and deal with your teen calmly. Avoiding power struggles is discussed in detail in Keys 6 and 22.

Maintain a Businesslike Approach. Some people will do things for you because of a relationship that has been formed or because you have been nice to them. Other people would see this willingness as a weakness that can be exploited and used. Suppose you have done ten favors for me in the past. One morning you ask me to drive you to pick up your car, which has been repaired. I am busy and do not want to take you, but ten flags pop up in my head and remind me of the favors that you have done for me and the fact that you have been very nice to me. Therefore, I say, "Come on, I'll take you. Where do we have to go?" Another personality type might think that he has "put something over" on the person ten times and say, "No, I can't take you. I am busy." Some people you can pay to paint your house before the job is done and you know the work will be completed. Others you would never pay until the job is finished; otherwise, it might never be completed. Most business contracts have rules that must be followed in order to receive the consequences. Never tell the teenager "I am going to get you a new fishing rod, and because I've gotten it for you, I want you to improve in school." It is better to say "We can get your new fishing rod as soon as you improve in school." The child needs rules or expectations and consequences spelled out ahead of time, and consequences should occur after she fulfills the expectation, not before. "You promised to cut the grass this afternoon. You will get your allowance after the grass is cut, not before."

Avoid Harsh, Lengthy, or Major Consequences. Some teenagers learn responsibility by repetition of consequences. For them, rather than have one big thing happen, it would be better if they experience twenty small consequences. Rather than taking away the phone for a month at a time, it might be better to take it away twenty times for one day. Severe, harsh, or lengthy punishments usually will work with the "attitude kid." For example, if you took away her phone privileges for a month, the attitude kid would go to her room every afternoon and think, "What a stupid thing I did. I can't talk to my friends. It's boring not to be able to talk on the phone." In other words, you would get her thinking about what she had done and the consequences she is experiencing. Using this approach with "attitude kids" can help to change their thinking pattern or to develop a new attitude. On the other hand, the "behavior kid" would miss the phone for the first day or two, then adapt to the situation and not talk on the phone or go down to the corner convenience store and use that phone.

Major, lengthy, or harsh consequences do not affect some teenagers. So failing a grade or having to go to summer school may not significantly change a behavior. Although a child may have to go to summer school, he nevertheless escapes doing homework dozens of times, and the major consequence of failing or going to summer school will not change his attitude about homework. It's better for this personality type to have the parent check with the teacher every Friday, and if the boy has completed all of his homework and class work, positive consequences follow. If he has not completed the work, a different consequence occurs. Using this approach a number of times a year is more effective than imposing one large consequence.

A "behavior kid" learns responsibility by repeated consequences. The more we can get him to do something, and something happens that he either likes or dislikes, the faster the behavior will change and an attitude will develop.

Big incentives or rewards that occur after a long period of time also do not work as well with the "behavior kid." At the beginning of the fall term, we may tell the teenager who has been slacking off his schoolwork, "If you have a B average by Christmas, we'll take you to Disney World for the holidays." Or, "If you do not get detention again for the rest of the term, we'll help you buy the mountain bike you want." If you offer this type of long-term incentive to some teenagers, they will work like crazy for three days after you spell out the expectation and consequence but will rapidly slide back into the old behavior. Or they will not show any behavioral change until three days before the report card, and then they will study twenty-four hours a day. For this particular personality type, it might be better to use a short-term goal such as weekend privileges, based on a report of his performance in school for the week. If you decide to use a long-term goal, you could also get a weekly report from school and he could earn points toward that goal on a weekly basis. In other words, the teenager having difficulty in school would receive points each week for completing homework and classwork, for paying attention in class, or for good behavior to avoid detention. If he has a certain amount of points at the end of the specified period, he can get his trip to Disney, his mountain bike, or another desired reward.

Avoid Giving Sentences. "Go to your room." "You're not allowed to watch television this weekend." "You can't use the phone for four weeks." "You will have to stay in after school for a week." These statements work well with some teenagers but not with others. Some adolescents serve the sentence, then do the same thing again. Sentences are primarily given to change an attitude and to get a teenager to think differently. Sentences work with the "attitude kid," but not with some other personality types.

Some teenagers work better toward things when there are goals or incentives. If you do give these youngsters a sentence, you want to put a light at the end of the tunnel; that is, a way they can work toward something or get out of the sentence. For example, rather than say, "Because you have been doing poorly in school, you cannot use the phone for four weeks," it would be better to explain, "You are grounded from using the phone for four weeks because you are doing poorly in school. However, each evening that you do your homework and do not give me any trouble, you will be able to talk on the phone that night." For some teenagers, if all you give is a sentence, the only thing that you can be sure will happen is that they will not talk on the phone and will serve the sentence. Their attitude toward homework or schoolwork will probably not improve. However, if you give them a sentence with a light at the end of the tunnel (a way to work out of the sentence), you may get a better response regarding their homework and schoolwork.

Avoid Excessive Explaining, Lectures, and Reasoning. Teenagers look forward to lectures about as much as we do to a heart attack. Many parents talk, explain, reason, and lecture too much. For some adolescents, this approach will not benefit in developing a better understanding of the situation nor will it help them to acquire responsible behaviors. Some teenagers will not accept explanations or reasons why they have to do something. One, five, fifty, or five hundred explanations will not satisfy them or make them understand. The only thing that will please them is what they want to hear. A teenager faced with a history test may ask, "Why do I have to study history? I'll never use it. It's dumb." After you offer numerous logical reasons and explanations of why history is an important subject, he is still objecting. The only thing that will satisfy him is for you to say, "Yes, you're right. History is dumb. Don't study for the test." However, you cannot respond in this fashion. Sometimes the only reason that it is necessary is "Because I said so."

Model Responsible Behaviors. We are very powerful models for our children. They learn both good and bad behaviors from watching us and seeing how we solve problems, deal with certain situations, or interact with people. If your teenager sees you acting in an irresponsible fashion or showing a lack of internal control, there is a strong probability that she will learn this type of behavior. Show her responsible actions.

Assign Chores. A large majority of parents feel that the performance of chores or duties around the house is a big part of developing responsibility. Giving a teenager duties around the house will not, by itself, develop responsibility, but it will help. When assigning tasks, you must state not only what you expect but what the consequences of failure to do the chores will be. There are several ways to do this.

An allowance may be based on chores. A teenager gets a certain amount of money for her allowance each week. Her jobs are to clean the cat's litter box every day and wash the dishes four times a week. Each time she does these chores without being told, she earns a portion of her allowance. If she does not do them without being told, she loses that portion of her allowance. Whether she gets the full allowance at the end of the week is totally her responsibility.

Another teenager's duty is to put his clothes away after they are placed on his bed. The rule might state, "I won't wash any more of your clothes until the clothes that have been placed on your bed are put away."

The adolescent's duty is to feed the dog, but she never does it without being told. Her mother might say, "You don't get your supper until the dog is fed." The natural consequence of not being responsible is that the teenager's supper is delayed and she may get hungry.

A youngster may be told, "If the bathroom is clean by noon, I'll drive you to your friend's house. If it is not clean by then, I'll have to clean it. Since that will give me more work and involve more of my time, I will not be able to drive you. You will have to walk to your friend's."

The use of logical or natural consequences can center around chores. You tell a child, "This is *our* house and we are *all* responsible for what has to be done in the house.

Your father has certain responsibilities, your sister has chores, I have many things to do to keep the house running, and you also have certain jobs. If you do not hold up your end and do not do what you are supposed to do, that means someone else will have to do it. When this happens, the other person has to use his or her time and energy to complete your responsibilities and will have less time and energy to do things for you." In other words, if the teenager cannot perform duties and tasks around the house to help other family members and make things easier for all involved, then the rest of the family will not do things for the teenager that will help him out or make things run more smoothly for him.

Chores can help develop self-discipline and responsibility, but they can also teach the adolescent to manipulate her parents if the parents do not consistently monitor the behavior. A teenager's chore is to clean her room before she leaves the house on Saturday. However, even though she does not always perform the task, she is still allowed to leave. If this happens, the parents are encouraging inappropriate behaviors and a lack of responsibility in the child.

In assigning chores, you must be very specific and define exactly what you mean by a clean room or a straightened kitchen. You must also specify the consequences of this behavior ahead of time. Your teenager's definition of a clean room may be different from yours, so it has to be clearly defined. See Key 9 for more information about this topic.

Once the rule and consequences are clearly spelled out, you should deal with a lack of compliance in a very calm and matter-of-fact way. For example, you tell your teenager, "You have to take out the trash by seven every night. If it is not taken out by then, I will take it out and you will not receive a portion of your allowance that day." If the chore is not completed, you should follow through with the specific consequence rather than nag, remind, lecture, or shout.

Distribute Chores Equally Among Siblings. If there are several children in the house, have them sit down and assign a weight or value to each chore. This will avoid arguments like, "I'm doing more work than my brother" or "My sister has an easier job than me." For example, the youngsters may decide that feeding the dog, emptying the dishwasher, and similar activities have a value of 1 point. Cleaning the table after meals, sweeping the kitchen, and similar activities are worth 2 points. Vacuuming, putting away clothes, and other jobs may have a value of 3 points. Cleaning the bathroom may be worth 4 points. By assigning different weights or values to activities, the children can feel that the system is fair and they are not doing more work than their siblings. If a child cleans the bathroom, which has a value of 4 points, another child may have to do four activities valued at 1 point each that day to equal his sister's work. Another way to create a fair situation among siblings when it comes to chores is to vary the activities. On a calendar you could write the child's name on the day he is supposed to do a particular chore. For example, if you have two children, Jason and Alan, and one of their chores is to feed the dog, you could alternate the initial J or A on the calendar every other day. When it came time to feed the dog, all you would have to do is look at the calendar to see whose day it is. By using this method, one child would not feel as if he has fed the dog ten times for every one time his brother completed the chore.

When, as a family, you establish the methods you'll use to share chores, set up at the start a time, place, and agenda for discussing how all of this is working.

Give an Allowance. An allowance is a fixed amount of money given to children on a periodic basis (weekly, biweekly, monthly). They could receive the allowance for doing nothing other than breathing or they could earn the allowance for performing household chores or duties. If an allowance system is put into practice in your home, base it on some type of work or behavior. It need not be a significant amount of work, but receiving the allowance should be contingent upon some type of behavior or job. An allowance system can often be used to help children develop responsibility or to teach them the value of money. However, there are several things that must be kept in mind when implementing such a system.

The range of incentives and rewards greatly decreases as children get older. For the adolescent, the range is somewhat small and often directly or indirectly involves money. When deciding whether an allowance should be used for a particular chore or be contingent on a certain level of cooperation or behavior, the first question that must be asked is, How important is money to the child? Some professionals feel that children should not receive money for certain behaviors, while others think it is all right. Some people feel that children should not be paid for things they are supposed to do. (Many of these concepts are discussed in Keys 11 and 12.) Money can be used as a reward or an incentive, but an allowance system is appropriate only if the teenager values or needs money. Some parents say they have instituted an allowance system but it does not work. In many cases, the reason for this is that the teenager does not care about money and to him one dollar is the same as one thousand dollars.

Another factor in deciding whether an allowance system should be implemented is "Does the teenager need money?" You tell a child that he will receive a $5.00-a-week allowance for putting out the garbage and walking the dog. He does not complete the chores and does not get the allowance. However, any time he is with you at the store and wants a soda, you buy it for him. At the shopping mall when he feels like playing a video game, you give him money to play. On Saturday you pay for him to go to a movie. Why does this child need his own money? He doesn't, because he is getting everything he wants. Whether he does the chores or not, he is still able to get the money he needs to fulfill his wants. A parent instituted an allowance system for her twelve-year-old daughter for performing chores around the home. The first week the allowance system worked beautifully, but after that it did not work. When the young girl was asked why she was not doing the chores, she said that any time she needed money she could go next door to her grandparents and they would give her all the money she needed. If an allowance system is used, you must dry up other sources of income in order to produce a need for money.

Another way to make the allowance system work is to specify certain activities or items that you will not pay for or purchase for the teenager. In other words, you tell the child that he will be given a certain allowance each week for doing certain duties. He is to use this money for going out on the weekend, buying gas for the car, playing video games, or anything else he wants. You will not pay for any of these material things or activities. If they are important items to the child, he will then need the allowance to pay for them himself.

The amount of allowance a child receives is based on two general factors: your financial situation and the needs of the teenager. However, it should be kept in mind that you can give too much allowance. This may create a situation where the teenager accumulates money. When he has enough, he does not have to work because the need for money does not exist. The purpose of the allowance system is thus defeated. You must assess the needs of the teenager and try to base the allowance accordingly. Naturally, a younger adolescent does not need as much spending money as an older one. What you expect a child to do with this money should be realistic. For example, it may be very difficult for a fifteen-year-old who receives ten dollars a week to use this allowance for both his lunch at school and movies on the weekend. Find out how much things cost today and try to become aware of your teenager's needs and the cost for him to fulfill these needs.

Be sure you and your child have the same idea of what is expected and what the consequences will be.

If the teenager does not earn the allowance, he should not receive it. If he earns the allowance, you must be certain that he receives it. You must be consistent. If you are inconsistent with payment of the allowance, the teenager may manipulate you or not complete the task or his motivation may decrease and his performance may be affected. If he performs the chores assigned, he should receive his allowance on a regular basis. In addition, you should never take away all or part of his allowance when the adolescent has earned it by completing his specific assignments. This will also decrease the effectiveness of the system. For example, a teenager has earned all of his allowance for helping around the house with various chores. On Friday when he is to receive his allowance, he comes home with a detention and because of the detention he is not given the total allowance. As a result, the next week when it comes to motivating him to do chores, he is probably not going to comply.

An allowance earned should be received. But be consistent and do not give the child the allowance if he has not earned it.

25

▼▼

REESTABLISHING TRUST

A lack of trust usually occurs when a child lies, lacks responsibility, or is manipulative or if generally you cannot believe that what he tells you is the truth or will actually happen. However, if you do not trust the adolescent and do not allow him the opportunity to earn back the trust, you will probably go on not trusting him for the rest of his life. Therefore, when trust has broken down in the parent-child interaction, certain things must be done to reestablish the trust. Part of reestablishing trust is to see more responsible behaviors displayed by the teenager.

Three components are involved in reestablishing trust. The teenager must first ask for a small privilege. Then the parent has to grant it. Finally, the teenager has to do exactly what he says he is going to do. The following example can be used with teenagers to illustrate a loss of trust:

Suppose you and your friend Jeff see each other every day. You go to school together or live in the same neighborhood. At least once a day Jeff asks you to lend him five, ten, or twenty-five cents and promises that he will pay you back tomorrow. Tomorrow comes and Jeff does not return the money. This goes on for six months, and he has not paid back one cent. Finally, one day Jeff asks, "Lend me a hundred dollars. I'll pay you back tomorrow." Ask the teenager, "What are you going to tell Jeff?" Most youngsters say something like,

"I'm not going to lend him the money." When asked "Why?" the usual response is, "Because he is not going to pay me back." When asked "Why do you feel that way?" they usually say, "I do not trust him. Jeff is saying one thing and doing something else." Examples of what the teens are doing at home can be used to explain that this is the same reason their parents either do not trust them or else question what they say.

The following three things have to happen in order to reestablish trust:

First, the teenager must realize that he cannot go to his parents and ask for unreasonable or big privileges or things. In other words, he should not ask to borrow a thousand dollars, because this is an unreasonable request. Instead, he has to start out by asking for some small privilege or request to be granted in order to begin rebuilding trust.

Second, the parents have to start granting the teenager's requests for small privileges. If they do not lend him the money he asks for or do not grant him some leeway and privileges, they will not have an opportunity to develop trust again.

Third, the teenager has to tell his parents something like, "I'll pay you back the money and I'll put it in the jewelry box in your bedroom." In order for the parents to develop trust, the youngster then has to put the money in the box, but, more importantly, the parents have to check that he has done so. Therefore, the third step in developing trust is that the teenager has to do what he says he is going to do and the parents have to check to see that he has done what he says.

I usually tell the teenagers that I know they manipulate their parents and sometimes lie or do not tell them the whole truth, but when they are trying to rebuild trust, they have to do exactly what they say they are going to do. In this way, trust will develop and they will be allowed more privileges. If an adolescent frequently complains to his parents, "You do not trust me. You never believe me. Why do you have to check up on me? Why do you have to call Robbie's mother to see that I am going to be at his house? Why do you have to check with the teacher to see if I am behaving in class when I say I am doing fine?" I advise his parents to tell the child, "If I do not check to see that you have done what you said you were going to do, there is no way I would be able to trust you." In other words, the reason I am checking on you is to develop trust. If I don't check to see if you went to Robbie's house, there would be no way to know that you are telling the truth and I still would not trust you. If I check and you are there, I will be able to begin reestablishing my trust in you.

If you use this approach, whether the teenager is given more privileges and freedoms will be completely his responsibility. If his behavior indicates he can be trusted, you can allow him more freedom or privileges. If his behavior does nothing to reduce your lack of trust, you will not give him additional freedom or privileges. In fact, if his behavior indicates that you must still question his ability to do what he says he is going to do, you might want to tighten up on him and to provide him with more restrictions. In other words, parents should try to put all of the responsibility onto the adolescent's shoulders, so that the amount and extent of what he does and how much trust is given to him is totally based on his behavior and his sense of responsibility.

26

‸‸‸

TRUST AND RESPONSIBILITY: THINGS TO REMEMBER

1. Although communication between parent and teenager is extremely important, children do not necessarily develop responsible attitudes and behaviors as a result of conversation or discussion. Some teenagers first have to be helped to establish the behavior (i.e., get in the habit of doing something) and then the attitude follows.

2. Avoid excessive lecturing, discussions, hollering, and other negative verbal interaction.

3. State the rule and the consequence of the behavior ahead of time. By doing this, you place the responsibility for his actions on the teenager's shoulders. If unpleasant things happen to him, he is the cause. Conversely, if good things happen, it is also his responsibility. Be sure to state the rule and the consequence at the same time. Avoid random disciplining and determining the consequence after a rule is broken. Tie the consequence directly to the behavior and make the teen responsible for his rewards and pleasures, as well as his punishments and disappointments. Avoid having things happen out of the

blue—that is, avoid dispensing punishments or rewards that have nothing to do with the adolescent's behavior.

4. Try to avoid power struggles and forcing the adolescent to perform certain tasks. If you battle the teenager to make him conform to your request, you are more responsible for the task being completed than he is.

5. Lose a few battles but win the war. In the beginning, the important thing in developing responsibility may be not that the task is completed but that the teenager experiences the consequences of his behavior and feels responsible for what happens to him. In some cases, getting the task accomplished may actually be the last thing the parent is trying to do. The first step is to make the youngster aware that there will be different consequences to his behavior. The second is to teach the adolescent that he is responsible for what happens to him. The third is to make the child aware that you will consistently follow through with what the teenager decides. The final thing you are trying to accomplish is to get the task completed. To reiterate: Getting the adolescent to complete the task is not as important as making him feel that he is responsible for what happens to him.

6. After the expectations and consequences are clearly stated and the teenager makes a decision that will result either in negative consequences or in not receiving positive consequences, he may try to blame others for what has happened: for example, "It's your fault that I didn't get my license" or "You're making me miss the dance on Friday night." If the adolescent uses this tactic, simply tell him, "It was your decision.

147

It's your responsibility. You knew what was going to happen to you before you did what you did. I'm only following through with what you told me to do."

7. Avoid lengthy, harsh, or major consequences. Rather than have one major consequence occur, it may be better if the youngster experiences twenty small consequences.

8. Meeting a teenager's every need or desire, giving her everything she wants, letting her have her way, spoiling her, and protecting her from experiencing the consequences of her behavior will usually interfere with the development of responsible behaviors.

9. Do not allow an adolescent to become excessively dependent on you, and do not assume responsibility for his behavior. This type of parent-child interaction makes it difficult for children to learn independent and responsible behaviors.

10. Giving a teenager duties and chores around the house will not by itself develop responsibility but it will help.

11. If an adolescent has behaved in a manner that causes you not to trust her, you must eventually give her the opportunity to reestablish the trust, by restoring some privileges and giving her some freedom. But the teenager then has to do what she says she is going to do in order for the trust to develop again. You may have to check up on her at times. Checking up does not necessarily mean that you do not trust your child, but that you are engaging in a behavior that will allow you to develop more trust in her.

27

~~~~~~

THE TELEPHONE— PROBLEM OR INCENTIVE?

A few activities that occur frequently in adolescents' lives are (1) spending time in their room, (2) being with friends or "going out," and (3) talking on the telephone.

Talking on the phone is part of the teenage ritual. If you have a teenager who does not spend or does not want to spend a considerable amount of time on the phone, he or she is the exception rather than the rule.

Problems That Arise. Problems that occur in the family because of the telephone usually stem from a few areas:

First, required activities do not get completed. Because adolescents spend so much time on the phone, they do not have time for homework, cleaning up their room, setting the table, helping with the dishes, or other normal tasks. Conflicts arise because the required duties or responsibilities are not completed.

Another problem arises because of the teenager's total involvement in his conversation to the exclusion of what is going on around him. Suppose that you have been working for two hours to clean the house and during that time your child has been lounging on her bed, talking on the phone. Shouldn't she be volunteering to help you instead of talking on the phone?

The third general area that causes some problems is that the teenager uses the phone too much or at the wrong time. Consequently, you can never use the phone when he is around, and your friends tell you that every time they call your house the line is busy.

The problems that arise from the use of the telephone are primarily the result of lack of structure—that is, a lack of rules regarding when, how long, and under what circumstances the phone may be used by the youngster. In order to minimize the difficulties that will occur regarding the phone and its usage, the parents must establish a set of rules and consistently enforce them.

Setting Rules and Consequences. Talking on the phone is a normal part of adolescence, and children should be allowed to do this, not only because it is a typical behavior, but because it tends to help socialization, the development of friends, and the ability to communicate and interact with other people. However, unless specific rules and consequences are set regarding this activity, problems are certain to arise. Keys 9 and 10 will give you some general ideas on how to set rules and consequences regarding use of the phone.

Just because a child has access to a phone does not mean that she has unlimited use of this privilege, just as having a driver's license does not mean that the teenager can use the car whenever he wants. The range and number of things that can serve as rewards, motivators, or incentives dramatically decreases when a child moves into the teenage years. The phone is one of the things that you can use as a motivator in order to get your teenager to show more appropriate, cooperative, and/or responsible behaviors. The Keys involving setting rules and consequences should be reviewed because they will give you some general ideas on how to accomplish this. A few examples follow.

Natural consequences. "I'm asking you to cooperate with me and stop aggravating your sister. You're asking me to cooperate with you and allow you to use my phone. If you cooperate with me, I'll cooperate with you. Any day that you do not cooperate with me, you will not be able to talk on the phone."

If a child has a phone in her room or her own phone line, you may decide to have her "pay" for this privilege. She may not actually have to give you real money, but she may have to "earn" money by doing chores, speaking nicely to her siblings, cooperating, etc. The amount she earns could be used to pay for daily or weekly phone service. The natural consequence of her not paying for the service is that the telephone will be disconnected.

To the teenager who is doing poorly in school because he is not putting forth effort or doing required work, you might say, "Your job is to go to school and do what you're supposed to do [homework, class work, paying attention, behaving in class]. If you are doing your job, you can have the privilege of talking on the phone. If you are not doing your job, you will not be allowed to use the phone." You then could get a weekly progress report from the school regarding the above behaviors.

Grandma's rule. "You can talk on the phone only after you have completed your homework." A child is having a problem with a particular subject, and you would like to help her review or study that subject each night rather than fight or nag the child. You might tell her, "The nights you show me your English homework and we can review it before seven

151

o'clock, you will be able to talk on the phone. The nights you do not show me the work, you will not be allowed to talk on the phone."

"You have four chores to complete every day after school. For each one you complete before eight o'clock, you will earn fifteen minutes of phone time. You can talk on the phone for an hour each night or not at all. It's up to you."

The point of these examples is that you may have to make your child earn phone time. By using the phone as an incentive, you may be able to modify an appropriate behavior or increase a desirable one. If you are considering putting a phone in a child's room or getting him his own private line, you could use this as a consequence and make him earn this privilege by changing some aspect of his behavior/attitude.

28

DRIVER'S LICENSE, DRIVING, AND USE OF THE FAMILY CAR

- At what age should a teenager get his driver's license?
- When should she be allowed to use the car alone?
- How frequently should my son drive?

These are frequent questions and concerns of parents of teenagers. It is difficult to give a specific answer to these questions, because each child is different, and driving and use of the car must be considered on an individual basis. Other factors besides age must be considered in arriving at the decision of when a teenager should be allowed to drive.

The major reasons parents are reluctant to let their adolescents drive center around two basic areas: immaturity and irresponsibility.

- She still acts like a child. How can I allow her to drive a car?
- His temper is so bad that I am afraid to allow him behind the wheel, because I don't know what would happen if he got angry while driving.
- He does not do what he is supposed to in regard to his schoolwork, so I do not have any confidence that he will do what he is supposed to while driving.

- Why should I let her have the privilege of driving when she does nothing around the house and I have to fight with her to get her to do the simplest thing, like picking up her clothes or cleaning up the kitchen after she eats?

In general, these parents are saying that the teenager shows behaviors that are more consistent with those of a younger child or that the adolescent is not showing the level of responsibility she should show for her age.

Other Factors, Not Age, Determine a Readiness to Drive. Maturity and responsibility are not time-acquired behaviors; that is, a child does not become mature at sixteen, eighteen, or twenty-one, nor does he acquire appropriate responsibility at a specific age. These behaviors are acquired through learning. If your child is not showing an appropriate level of maturity or responsibility for his age, he has not learned them.

Maturity. In general, maturity means behaving or possessing skills appropriate for one's age. There are five general areas of maturity.

- Physical. This area pertains to the development of physical skills. A child might be ten years old but show the fine-motor coordination of a seven-year-old. Therefore, he may have some problems writing or manipulating a pencil when it comes to performing at a fifth-grade level. Physical immaturity may also involve gross motor coordination or other physical attributes.

- Academic. This refers to the development of skills that are necessary in the academic setting. A child may be in fifth grade but reading on a third-grade level. A lack of academic maturity may also pertain to some intellectual deficits (e.g., a slow learner).

154

- Social. This pertains to the development of age-appropriate skills required to interact with other children. A child may be fifteen, but his social development is similar to that of a ten-year-old.

- Emotional. This pertains to emotional reactions to situations. A thirteen-year-old still has temper tantrums. The twelve-year-old may whine when he does not get his way. The thirteen-year-old cries when faced with a problem. In general, their emotional reaction to situations is not consistent with their age but more similar to that of a younger child.

- Behavioral. This involves behavior factors such as responsibility, attention span, concentration. The child is fifteen, yet the parents still have to fight with him to do his homework.

The levels of maturity that usually relate to ability to function adequately behind the wheel of a car involve the last two areas, emotional and behavioral.

Responsibility. Responsibility generally means doing what you have to do because you *have* to do it, not because you *want* to do it. It involves duties, chores, and other tasks. On the part of the teenager, it may involve schoolwork, picking up after himself, taking care of his room, coming home on time, and many other similar behaviors. Key 24 explains in detail how to develop responsibility. It should be reviewed before proceeding any further.

Helping the Teenager Develop Appropriate Behavior. If you have a teenager whose emotional attitude and behavior are not at a level that would allow you to trust him and let him get a driver's license or use the car, there are several things that can be done to help build this trust.

Responsible or mature behaviors seen in one area may allow you to have more confidence in a child in a totally different area. For example, let's say you have two neighbors. One neighbor takes care of his house, cuts the grass, repairs things when broken, and generally shows a great deal of pride and concern for his house. Your other neighbor very seldom cuts the grass, leaves his house in disrepair, and has a lot of trash in his backyard. You have a car that you have a great deal of attachment to and value highly. Both of these people come to you and ask you to borrow this valued possession. Which neighbor would you trust with the car? Although neither one of these people has ever borrowed your car before, the behavior they show in other areas of their lives enables you to trust one more than the other.

Many times with teenagers you can use other areas in their lives to help you develop enough trust or confidence in them to allow them to get a license and drive.

Specify the Behaviors. Try to stay away from general concepts like, "You will be able to drive when you do better in school," "You will get your driver's license when you show me more responsibility," or "When you act your age, I will consider allowing you to get behind the wheel of a car." Your definition of doing better in school, showing more responsibility, and acting one's age is probably different from your teenager's. Be very specific and map out exactly what the child has to do in order to obtain the goal. Avoid broad, general concepts. Following are several examples of behavioral problems and methods of dealing with them:

1. Poor school performance. An adolescent is doing poorly in school because she is not doing what she is supposed to do (homework, class work, paying attention in class). This child already has her driver's license, but you do not feel that her level of responsibility in school warrants the use of the car.

You might want to set up a weekly communication system with the school to monitor her behavior and performance. Under this system, you obtain weekly progress reports from her teacher regarding the completion of homework and class work and her behavior or attention in class.

The child can earn a total of thirty points for the week for perfect performance. You might tell her that fifteen points will get her the use of the car one day during the weekend, twenty points will get her two days, and anything over twenty-five will allow her to use the car the entire weekend. By using a method like this, you have shown the teenager exactly what "doing better in school" means, and if she wants to use the car, she knows what she has to do in order to obtain this privilege.

2. Problems with temper. Another child wants to obtain his driver's license but has difficulty controlling his temper. He also becomes easily upset and agitated when things do not go as planned or expected, when he is faced with obstacles, or when he does not get his way. Because of this behavior, you question how he would respond behind the wheel of a car if he became upset. Therefore, in order for you to gain more confidence in allowing him to get a driver's license, this behavior would have to improve.

You would very specifically define the behavior that you want to eliminate: "When you get angry, you usually start screaming or throwing things. Each week that you do not show these behaviors, you will earn a point. When you get ten points you may get your permit and you can take driver's education. After that happens, each week that you do not show these behaviors we will be able to practice driving for half an hour on Sunday. When you have accumulated six hours of driving time, I will let you take the test for your license." After the driver's license is obtained, use of the car could also be determined on a weekly basis by the adolescent's ability to control his temper.

3. Irresponsibility around the house. This particular teenager, for example, does not pick up after himself or has to be told many times to clean his room or straighten up the bathroom. A child displaying this kind of behavior could earn driving privileges by showing more responsibility at home. You could specifically define what you mean by responsibility and set up a chart or keep a record of the child's behavior during the week. A similar procedure could be used as follows.

For example, a child may be able to use the car for a total of eight hours a week. Responsibility for this child could be defined as taking care of his belongings, putting things where they belong, cleaning up after himself, and so on. This could be put on a chart. Every time the child leaves his shoes in the den, does not clean the kitchen after he eats, leaves the bathroom a mess, or performs any other behavior that has been previously defined, a mark could be placed on the chart. For every mark that was received during the week, he would lose fifteen minutes of driving time. If he received twenty marks during the week, he would only be able to use the car for three hours the following week.

Similar procedures, involving a driver's license or use of the car, could be used to modify behaviors such as fighting with siblings, insolence, or coming home on time.

Using Driving as an Incentive or a Motivator. Since driving seems to be vitally important to most teenagers, parents can use this as a motivator. This reward can actually be broken into four separate areas. Each area could be a goal and certain behaviors could be required to attain each goal.

- Taking the written test and obtaining a learner's permit. In most states both a written test and actual driving test must be successfully completed in order to obtain a driver's license. If the adolescent passes the written test, she can then obtain a learner's permit, which allows her to drive with a licensed adult in the car. Once she has a learner's permit, the next incentive could be employed.

- Driving practice. The child's behavior during the week determines the amount of practice driving time she has on the weekend with her mother or father. The more cooperation she displays during the week, the longer the time she will have to practice driving.

- Taking the driving test. Once the teen has gained some driving skill, and her behavior continues to indicate that she is responsible or mature enough to handle driving, then you can allow her to take the driving test. After passing the test, the child is issued a driver's license.

- Using the car. Although the child has her driver's license, this does not necessarily mean she has unlimited use of the car. The amount of time that you allow her to use the car during the week or on the weekend could also be contingent on her behavior. If she continues to show responsible or mature behaviors in the areas that you specify, privileges could be extended. However, if the behaviors she improved to obtain the license start to diminish, you could restrict the privileges. Privileges to use the car would be granted if most of the work was completed in school, or they could be restricted or denied if the required effort was not shown.

Insurance, Gas, and Maintenance. Nowadays, a significant amount of cost is incurred if a parent decides to allow the child to use the family car. Insurance costs are high, especially if your adolescent is a male. Extra expenses for gas and maintenance are also likely to be incurred.

Whether or not the teenager should be responsible for these expenses is an individual decision and is dependent upon the family's financial situation and personal values, among other things. Some parents feel that a teenager's job is to go to school and do what he is supposed to do, and if that occurs they will be more than happy to pay for the extra insurance, gas, or repairs. Other parents feel that the child should earn the money himself. Some families cannot afford the higher cost of insurance or gasoline if a teenager drives; therefore, the child must earn the money to be able to drive.

Whether or not the family can afford the extra insurance, gas, and maintenance costs, a child should not receive the valuable privilege of driving the car in exchange for breathing. This privilege should be earned. It may not be that in order to drive, the child has to earn the actual amount of the insurance increase involved, but he may be required to show a certain level of cooperation in the home to obtain car privileges. Another child could be required to show adequate performance in school in order for his parents to continue to pay for the added insurance cost and gas.

Drinking and Driving. *Enough emphasis cannot be placed on not driving when drinking.* Parents can obtain valuable literature on this subject from M.A.D.D. (Mothers Against Drunk Driving), which could be shared with their teenager. Because of the seriousness of this situation and the potential danger involved, driving while under the influence of alcohol/drugs should carry a severe restriction of driving privileges.

Conclusion. Being able to earn a driver's license and drive are powerful motivators during adolescence. They can be used to the parent's positive advantage. Use of the car and driving privileges should be based on behavior, not age. Try to look for responsible and mature behaviors that indicate the child is capable enough to handle this privilege. If you feel that you cannot trust the child to drive because he is not showing appropriate behaviors in other areas, spell out exactly what he must do to earn this privilege. Monitor his behavior and give or take away the privilege *consistently*. He should know exactly what he has to do in order to obtain his driver's license or use the car. He should also know what he must or must not do in order to be restricted from these privileges.

29

~~~~~~

DRUG AND ALCOHOL ABUSE AMONG ADOLESCENTS

L et's say we stop the first adolescent who passes by your house. I give him money and tell him to purchase some illegal drugs. At the same time, I give you money and tell you to get me a six-pack of soda. Both of you would probably get back at the same time with the items I requested.

This is an exaggeration, but not far from the truth. Drugs are available everywhere, from the highest socioeconomic levels to the lowest, from the best schools to the poorest schools. Recent surveys by national organizations related to drug abuse and alcoholism show:

1. The average age of first drug use is thirteen. The average age of first alcohol use is twelve.

2. Over 50% of high-school seniors have tried drugs. Over 33% have tried a drug other than marijuana.

3. Nearly 33% of all high school seniors claim that most of their friends get drunk at least once a week.

4. Nearly one in sixteen has tried cocaine or its powerful, addictive derivative, crack.

5. High school senior girls ingest more stimulants and tranquilizers than boys. Girls almost match the boys' use of alcohol, marijuana, and other drugs.

6. Approximately 33% of fourth graders reported peer pressure to try alcohol and marijuana.

Times Have Changed. Things have changed dramatically since we were children. The drug user or addict in our day was seen as a degenerate. Today, drug use cuts across all socioeconomic levels. It is even seen on TV and in movies as something done at social gatherings or parties. Negative effects are minimized.

Attitudes and values of the adolescent and preadolescent have shifted away from authority figures and toward more pleasure-seeking, big-money, fast-living people— toward sex, drugs, alcohol, and money.

This Key gives a general overview of substance abuse in preadolescents and adolescents and touches on types of situations in which substance abuse is more likely to occur and reasons for this behavior. Signs and symptoms of substance abuse are also included. For further details, consult one of the many excellent books on this subject. Also, check with the substance abuse agency in your area, which can provide literature about drug and alcohol use.

Why Use Drugs? There are many theories on the causes of substance abuse. They range from a genetic basis to personality characteristics. Drug or alcohol abuse in children usually seems to be a symptom of confusion, unhappiness, or alienation. Let's look at four general areas of characteristics often seen in these children.

• Lack of self-discipline. Children who lack self-discipline often show a lack of internal control and responsibility.

163

They have a self-centered, pleasurable approach to the environment and feel little personal or social responsibility. These youngsters are often impulsive, act before they think, and have difficulty adhering to duties and responsibilities imposed by others. Trouble with authority figures is frequent and they show poor academic performance because of a lack of responsibility. They often set very high goals for themselves but do not have the self-discipline or knowledge of the process necessary to achieve these goals. An example is a child who tells me he is going to go to law school, make a lot of money, and own a big home and expensive cars. However, the reason he's in my office talking to me is that he wants to quit high school. Youngsters like this know how to set goals but don't know how to achieve them.

- Lack of motivation. Some teenagers appear to lack interest in activities, things, and events. They show a disinterest in school and do not have any hobbies. They live day to day and moment to moment. They show little or no interest in or put no value on personal achievement or success. They don't plan ahead or show any concern for future events or consequences they may experience.

- Unhappiness, dissatisfaction, depression, anxiety, boredom. These are frequent symptoms in teenagers who have a negative picture of themselves and see others as better than they are. They generally lack confidence in their abilities. They are unhappy in their home setting and often feel alienated and not part of their family unit.

- Socialization problems. Teens with socialization problems usually maintain friendships on a superficial level or else do not have many friends. Often they do not have a close friend and feel isolated from their peers. They have trouble with authority, difficulties at home, and conflicts with family members. They are easily influenced by peers.

164

These characteristics are typical but not conclusive. Adolescents who abuse drugs or alcohol have different personality characteristics and different reasons for using them. Below are some of the most frequent reasons for this behavior.

- Experimentation. Almost all teenagers try alcohol or drugs. If the child is only experimenting, this behavior will be seen very infrequently or observed a few times, then discontinued. Experimentation is the first stage in the four steps toward substance dependency. It is usually followed by occasional use, which is less than once a week, then regular use, where the child is actively involved with drinking or drugs. The final stage is dependence.

- Peer pressure. All the teenager's friends are involved with drugs or alcohol. He may not be able to go against the influence or pressure of the peer group.

- Rebellion. Sometimes drug or alcohol use is based on the child's tendency to rebel against parental or societal values.

- Confidence problems. Teenagers with negative self-concept are often insecure and lack confidence. This may be the basis of some drug and alcohol usage.

- To promote and enhance social interaction. Some teenagers who have difficulty interacting with agemates or the opposite sex feel that drugs or alcohol releases inhibitions and make it easier for them to relate to peers.

- To mask depressive feelings. Some teenagers use drugs or alcohol as self-medication. Their emotional difficulties center around depression, hopelessness, and unhappiness. These substances seem to help alleviate the symptoms.

- They like it. Some teens are involved because drinking or using drugs makes them feel good and they enjoy the pleasurable feeling of getting high.

165

Signs and Symptoms of Substance Abuse. There are many symptoms of substance abuse. The list that follows is not conclusive. If your child shows one or two of the symptoms, it doesn't mean he is using drugs or alcohol. Be concerned when you observe a cluster of symptoms. Look first for symptoms you can see. Often, appearance is affected by the use of drugs or alcohol.

• Seeing the child drunk. The child is drunk frequently. Alcohol or medications disappear from the home. You find hidden drugs or alcohol. You discover store-bought drug paraphernalia (packets of rolling paper, various types of pipes, syringes). You frequently find household items that may be used as drug paraphernalia (plastic bags, baggies, lock-type pouches, aluminum-foil strips, small bottles, boxes, razor blades, weighing scales, kitchen spoons, and bottle caps burnt black on the bottom).

• Loss of interest. Loss of ambition. Loss of interest in hobbies, sports, or activities. Overall deterioration of morals or values.

• Physical changes. Deterioration in health and/or physical appearance. Appetite swings, either a loss or an increase. Bloodshot eyes, hyperactivity, frequent "colds" or nosebleeds.

• Personality changes. The child doesn't seem to like himself. Mood swings. Violent or destructive behavior. Severe depression. Threats of suicide or actual attempts. Running away from home or threats to run away.

• Loss of interest in school. Grades start to drop. Missing school.

• Secretive behavior. The door to his room is locked. Very private phone calls. Chronic tardiness (late for school, dates, activities).

• Avoidance of others. Avoiding family functions, neighbors, or old friends. Hanging out with older children. Verbal and/or physical abuse of parents or siblings. Changes in friends or hangouts.

- Money problems. Money disappearing from the house. Vague money needs. Sudden expenses. The child has money but you don't know where it is coming from.

- Chronic lying. Frequent alibis, excuses, and justifications (Teachers don't like me. Everybody is picking on me. You don't understand me.). Inability to keep promises. Excuses, such as: Everyone smokes (or drinks). Why should you care? It's not hurting you.

- Trouble with police. Police involvement of any kind. Driving-under-the-influence citations. Automobile or motorcycle accidents.

Dealing with Substance Abuse

- Contact a mental health professional. If you suspect substance abuse in your child, contact a mental health professional who specializes in this area. Not all mental health professionals have this expertise, so be sure you contact one who has training and experience. See Key 31. Most communities have substance abuse centers that offer treatment or can provide you with additional information.

- Identify and alleviate problems. Problems may be related to school, family, or peers, as well as to the child himself. If there is marital conflict in the home, discipline problems with the child, school failure, or socialization problems, try to resolve these.

- Encourage new friendships. This is more difficult to do with an adolescent than a younger child, but try to help him establish new friendships. Don't put down, criticize, or talk negatively about his current friends, because when you do that, the child feels you are talking about him. At times it may be appropriate to restrict friendships. Rather than restricting, however, it is better to encourage new friendships.

- Encourage the development of new interests. Provide opportunities for the child to develop hobbies, interests, and activities.

- Build confidence. Accentuate positive attributes and look for areas in the child's life that may produce a lack of confidence. Do things to counteract the latter and enhance a positive self-image.

- Develop overall responsibility and self-discipline. Many children are unmotivated and show problems with responsibility. They don't weigh consequences; this may be part of the problem with substance abuse. Try to develop overall responsibility in areas revolving around the home (chores, keeping their room clean) and with school.

- Establish communication. Most adolescents tend to withdraw from their families and not communicate as much with their parents at this age. Many times when professionals talk to adolescents about drugs or alcohol and try to make a point, children see this as a lecture or some type of reprimand. Try to establish an open line of communication with your child. Talk to her about her interests, likes, and dislikes. At times, the goal of communication is not to gather information, but to interact and exchange information in a positive manner. See Keys 18 through 20.

- Don't be manipulated. Many substance abusers are skilled at manipulation. Don't overextend your trust and allow yourself to be manipulated. Establish rules and consequences to follow. Do things to help you build trust in the youngster.

- Eliminate inappropriate models. If you suspect drug or alcohol abuse in your child, be sure you aren't modeling similar behaviors for him. The models for this behavior may be occurring in your home, with his peers, on television, or in the movies.

- Treat emotional problems. If your child experiences emotional difficulties (depression, unhappiness, anxiety), see an appropriate mental health professional.

- Set rules and consequences for behavior. Avoid protecting the child from consequences or rescuing him. Establish definite rules and consequences. Certain events should follow consistently if the child shows specific behaviors, especially continued drug or alcohol abuse.

30

~~~~~~

DEALING WITH SUICIDE

The incidence of suicide in children and adolescents has nearly tripled over the past twenty years. Some suicides are based on impulse, but most are planned and given much thought and long consideration. There is no single answer as to why a young person wishes to end his or her life, but research tends to point to such factors as family problems and pressures, loss of a loved one or important relationship, identity problems, availability of drugs and alcohol, high academic competition, and needs and goals that are not accessible. While it is difficult to say what type of child will attempt suicide because it is prevalent in all types of young people, the child who is isolated, aloof, and no trouble to anyone is more likely to attempt this than others. These children often need attention but do not get it at home or school because their behavior does not demand it. They do not stand out and are easily overlooked. While it is difficult to provide personality characteristics of the child who will attempt suicide, there are many clues and signs that one can look for. The more symptoms the child shows, the higher the risk.

Danger Signs or Characteristics. The signs or characteristics that will help identify and prevent a possible suicide attempt can be divided into three general areas: verbal, behavioral/feelings, and situational.

Verbal characteristics

All statements revealing a desire to die should be taken seriously.

1. Direct communications:
   "I'm going to kill myself."
   "I want to die."
   "I want to be with Grandpa in Heaven."
   "I wish I were dead"
   "I'm going to shoot myself."

2. Indirect communications:
   "You won't have to worry about me much longer."
   "Everyone would be better off without me here."
   "I'm causing all the problems in the family."
   "I can't take the pressure much longer."
   "I'm a burden to my parents."
   "My friends don't need me. All I do is cause trouble."

Behavioral/feelings characteristics

Changes in behavior or personality and the emergence or presence of certain feelings and attitudes may indicate a suicidal personality.

1. Withdrawal. The child becomes more of a loner and isolates himself from others or activities. Socialization with his peers and verbal interaction with others decreases. He may appear deep in thought much of the time and unaware of others.

2. Depression, crying, unhappiness, and apathy, as well as feelings of hopelessness, helplessness, and use-lessness.

3. Anxiety, confusion, agitation, moodiness, or other signs of disturbance.

4. A decline in academic performance.

171

5. An increase in sleeping or an inability to sleep.

6. An increase or a decrease in appetite.

7. Preoccupation with or questions about death, dying, religion, deceased relatives, Heaven, etc.

8. Making final arrangements or trying to "get [his] affairs in order." This may involve giving away treasured personal possessions (e.g., stereo, baseball glove, CD collection), paying back debts, doing favors for those he has mistreated, keeping a diary or excessive writing, organizing his belongings.

9. Recent involvement with drugs or alcohol.

10. Lack of optimism or hope about the future.

11. Neglect of appearance.

Situational characteristics
Certain situations or environmental conditions are common with children who attempt suicide.

1. Previous suicide attempts or threats.

2. A history of counseling, therapy, or psychiatric hospitalization.

3. Problems or chaos in the family. Disorganized home or breakdown of family structure (e.g., death, divorce, separation).

4. Pressure from the family to be successful. The teenager feels that he must be perfect to please his parents.

5. Dissatisfaction with the home situation, rules, or restrictions, and a feeling that things will not change

because his parents' rules, behavior, reactions, and actions are etched in stone.

6. The feeling that the teenager's family does not understand, respect, or appreciate him. The adolescent's feelings of unhappiness, frustration, or failure are unacceptable to the parents. Parental rejection.

7. Physical fights with others and/or family members. Physical and assaultive behavior in family members.

8. Increased tension, pressure, competitiveness, and demands from school and/or peers. Failure in school.

9. Loss of a loved one or close, important relationship.

10. Adolescent identity problems. Transition from adolescence to adulthood.

11. Suicide plans that involve highly lethal or quick methods (e.g., gunshot, hanging, jumping off a bridge). Suicide plans are specific with the details well worked out.

12. Recent suicide of a friend, relative, or admired person.

While it is difficult to identify a "suicide personality," the more of the above signs or characteristics the teenager shows, the higher the risk. Whether the suicide attempt is impulsive or well thought out, a lack of optimism, a sense of unhappiness, and a lack of hope about the future are usually present.

What to Do? If a teenager is making verbal comments indicating a desire to die, that situation should get your attention and you should take his threat seriously. The first thing you should do is to identify the situation or circumstances when this feeling is expressed. Does it occur when the child does not get his way (e.g., when you do not buy him something he requests or when you will not let him go to a dance or concert)? Does it occur after you punish him or when making you feel guilty will be to his advantage? Is he trying to get a reaction out of you or make you upset? Can you predict when you will hear him say this? Or does it occur in an unpredictable situation, such as watching TV, riding in the car, or in a conversation about school or his friends? How frequently does it occur and under what circumstances?

Some comments about suicide are manipulative and can be viewed and reacted to in a similar fashion as "I hate you," "You're mean," "I'm running away," or "I want to live at Grandma's." This would be especially true if the child has a manipulative personality. Have the child express his feelings and discuss them, but stay calm; do not allow the child to manipulate you.

Whether the expression concerning a desire to die is predictable or not or is seen as manipulative or not, the next step is to look for possible danger signs or characteristics. If you can identify several of the above feelings, behavioral changes, or situations in your child, I would take the remark very seriously. The more frequently you hear the comments, the more seriously you should regard them. Talk to the child about his feelings and about suicide. Do not offer simple answers to serious problems or tell the child all of the reasons he should not feel the way he does. This may increase his feelings of guilt and make him feel more worthless and hopeless. Try to understand his feelings and have him generate other solutions to the problem(s). When in doubt or when you have unanswered questions, get in touch with a mental health professional who specializes in children and adolescents so that he or she can provide you with assistance.

174

31

DO YOU NEED
PROFESSIONAL HELP?

Parents who are considering interventions by a mental health professional may be thinking, "Is my child's behavior normal or abnormal?" "Should I be concerned about this?" "Is this typical for his age?" "Can we deal with this behavior, attitude, or problem by ourselves?"

If your teenager is having trouble at home, at school, in the neighborhood, with his teachers, or with his friends, and it seems that this behavior is not typical for his age group, then you may want to consider professional intervention. If the teacher, coach, or some other person involved with your child is telling you something is unusual, listen. In order to determine if the behavior should be of further concern, you need to assess if it is normal. This is discussed in great detail in Keys 2 through 4.

If you assessed the situation and feel that you do not have the skills to cope with or evaluate it and/or you feel the behavior is not normal, then you need to locate someone who can provide you with the necessary evaluation, treatment, or information.

Locating a Competent Professional. When trying to locate someone to provide mental health services, be sure the individual has the proper credentials (i.e., license, certification). You would also want to determine if he or she has the expertise in the type of counseling, information, and evaluation that you need. Regardless of the profession (psychology, psychiatry, or social work) of the person you select to work with you and your child, I would suggest that you choose someone who primarily deals with children/adolescents. If I need heart surgery, I am not going to seek a general surgeon who performs brain surgery, cataract operations, and heart operations. I want someone who only works on hearts and specializes in heart surgery. Similarly, I would not want someone to see my thirteen-year-old who also does marriage counseling, sees geriatric patients, and works with hospitalized adults. I want a professional who primarily works with children and adolescents.

The best way to locate a competent professional is to ask the people who work with adolescents to make some recommendations—perhaps the child's teacher, principal, counselor at school, or pediatrician. If you ask several people, you will probably hear the same name a few times and this may give you some indication of the respect for or competency of that person. Other parents may have also sought mental health services, and they could give you some idea of what they thought about the person who worked with their child. I would be very hesitant about people who offer fad treatments or who make many claims of success and provide guarantees. Competent individuals usually do not have a need to advertise; therefore I would also stay away from agencies or individuals who extensively use the media to advertise their services. The person with the largest ad in the telephone book is not necessarily the most competent in that profession. He or she has just spent the most money on advertising in the book. Ask professionals in your area, your child's doctor, your doctor, and other people whose opinion you respect to provide you with some names.

32

CABLE TV, VIDEO GAMES, AND THE COMPUTER

Years ago a typical complaint from parents was "All my child wants to do is watch TV or listen to music. He does not do much with children his age and stays inside too much." Today the complaints are similar, but the radio, TV, and stereo have been replaced with video games, cable TV, and the computer. There is nothing inherently wrong or bad with the above electronic instruments; however, problems arise when they are used excessively or without proper supervision. Problems that occur are seen in several areas.

A lack of supervision of these activities not only results in excessive involvement in these activities, but may also result in the child coming in contact with information and activities that are age-inappropriate and that can be sexually explicit and/or involve violence. Concerns related to this are discussed in the Keys on violence in the schools and the Internet.

Some children spend most of their waking hours outside of school watching TV, playing video games, or on the computer. Excessive involvement with these activities generally results in problems in two areas.

First, required activities are neglected or get partially completed. Homework may not be done and grades decline. Chores around the house and other responsibilities may not be completed. As a result of this, parents may not allow their child to become involved in watching TV or playing video games. However, if you prohibit a child from watching TV, playing video games, or getting on the computer for not doing homework, the only thing we are sure of is that he will not be involved in this activity. There is no assurance that he will do homework. A better way to accomplish your goal is to restrict the activity and use it as an incentive to get the work done. For example, playing video games would be contingent on a behavior (completing homework, having a clean room). Read Key 27, on the telephone, which discusses several ways of accomplishing this.

The second problem that occurs is a reduction of socialization experiences and peer interaction. Eventually this means a minimal number of or even no friends or peer involvement. To teenagers, being with friends and social activities are a major part of their lives. A child with minimal social involvement has a big void in his life, and many teenagers are unhappy with this. A teenager with no social life who is not motivated about school or is unhappy because all he does is go to school and watch TV is difficult to motivate, and it is difficult helping him to modify his behavior. A child with an active social life who shows similar problems is much easier to deal with. Therefore, we would want to increase the isolated child's opportunity for socialization experiences and reduce the amount of time he is involved with video games, TV, and the computer. Use of these devices would be contingent on his involvement with other children. For example, the amount of time spent playing video games would be based on the amount of time spent outside the house or with peers. He would be allowed access to the computer if he joined an activity involving agemates (youth groups, school clubs, sports). Key 9, on setting rules and consequences, discusses several methods to accomplish this.

The use of video games, TV, and computers must be monitored and should be only one aspect of the teenager's life—not a major part.

33

⌃⌃⌃

THE INTERNET

Involvement with the Internet could result in problems related to excessive use, exposure to information that is not age-appropriate, and giving away personal information that may put the teenager or his family at risk. Unacceptable relationships with members of a marginal subculture, individuals with emotional problems, or older people is also common. Problems pertaining to excessive use were discussed in Key 32, on cable TV, video games, and the computer.

The second group of problems is primarily related to a lack of parental supervision. Although the Internet contains a wealth of information that can be very helpful to the teenager in school, it can also provide teenagers with information that can be detrimental. For example, the teenagers who committed recent killings in a high school learned how to make bombs on the Internet. Guns can be purchased on-line. Pornography and very explicit sexual pictures are available on the Internet. Teenagers could be exposed to hate messages that promote violence. The Internet does not discriminate between fact and fantasy or truth and lies. It provides all types of information. Teenagers could easily be given inaccurate information to be used in school assignments or to share with their peers. Since numerous things can be purchased on-line, shopping sprees and gambling are possible using the parent's credit cards. Teenagers could also provide legitimate businesses or crooks with personal information (address, phone number, credit card numbers, Social

Security number) about themselves or their parents that may prove detrimental.

Leaving a child alone with the TV on may expose him to sex and violence. On the Internet the major danger is not the sex and violence but the people the teenager could meet online. If unsupervised, teenagers can be easy prey for sexual predators. Children have been known to develop "relationships" and "fall in love" with individuals who were ten to fifteen years older than they, who they met and communicated with on the Internet. Teenagers can be exposed to people and information that are not consistent with the values and attitudes of some parents and what some people would feel to be appropriate.

The solution to this problem seems fairly simple— parental supervision. Some teenagers require more supervision and structure than others. For example, you could tell your daughter "come home at a reasonable time" and she will come home at a reasonable time. You tell your other child the same thing and he will come home in two weeks and argue with you that this is a reasonable time. With the self-disciplined, responsible child you could say "Don't turn on the computer when I'm not home" and he will listen. Another child will turn the computer on as soon as you leave the house. You probably have a pretty good idea about your children—who can be trusted or is more responsible and who is not. Self-disciplined, responsible children are easy to supervise—they listen, cooperate, and comply with authority. Stubborn, strong-willed, manipulative, and/or irresponsible teens are more difficult to supervise. Most of the following discussion pertains to this type of child.

The more difficult child is usually irresponsible in many aspects of his life (homework, keeping his room clean, for example) and does not listen to authority in a number of areas (such as getting off of the phone at a certain time, doing chores, coming home on time). The parent's first job with this child is not to make him responsible with the computer and Internet, but to make him more responsible in as many areas of his life as possible. Refer to previous Keys dealing with responsibility.

Placing the computer in an area of the house that usually contains adults or is a high traffic area would help monitor what is being done on the Internet. Limit or restrict solo surfing. If the Internet is required for school assignments and reports, the teenager could wait for the parent to assist him when access is needed. The parent could be with him when he surfs the Internet and downloads the sites he needs.

Screening software can be helpful. It is not foolproof, but it will filter some of the unacceptable material. Some Internet service providers offer their own screening systems. Screening software can black out undesirable information and web sites. Someone who knows about computers could give you information or programs that would allow you to block access to certain sites or provide techniques to help determine what was done on the computer that day.

Setting specific guidelines (don't talk to strangers, don't give personal information, don't use your real name, don't order anything without permission, don't post photos of yourself) is needed. Clear limits and rules need to be set along with specific consequences for compliance and noncompliance.

Teenagers also have access to the Internet outside of the home. The school or library may have methods to prevent the child from being exposed to inappropriate material. In general, you would not let your child sleep at a friend's house or spend a weekend with a family until you got to know the parents. The same thinking should be used when allowing a child to visit a friend with access to the Internet.

For all the dangers that exist on the Internet, keeping children away from it can be difficult. You need to communicate with your children and get involved in their lives to know their interests, attitudes, friends, and so on. Clear rules and consequences need to be set pertaining to use and misuse of the Internet. Attempts need to be made to develop responsibility and trust in all areas of your teenager's life. Supervision is absolutely necessary, with the amount of supervision dependent on the child's personality. For some children, explaining the "do's" and "don't's" is all that will be necessary. For others, taking the keyboard to work with you may be needed to provide adequate supervision.

With appropriate supervision, access to the Internet can be used as an incentive or consequence that can be used to motivate teenagers or help modify their behavior. See the suggested readings for a book related to this topic.

34

▲▲▲

VIOLENCE IN
THE SCHOOLS

In recent years, guns and shootings in schools, as well as children committing serious violence against other children, have become more of a national concern. Some people blame video games, violence on TV, guns, and so on; however, a primary cause of this violence is a lack of parental supervision or involvement in their child's life. The teenagers who did the shooting and killings in a suburban high school learned to make bombs over the Internet and the parents were not aware of this. The six-year-old who brought a gun to school and killed another six-year-old appeared to be from a very unstructured home situation with minimum supervision. This lack of supervision does not always result from parental neglect. It is also related to the time factor. In many families, both parents work and the children are shuffled to and from before- and after-school care. Conversely, teenagers are often home alone until the parents come home from work. Overall, the amount of time the parents are around their children and involved in providing supervision seems significantly different than it was as little as fifteen years ago.

As mentioned in Keys 32 and 33, on cable TV and the Internet, parental supervision and involvement must be present in order to minimize an adolescent's exposure to inappropriate media. You have to talk to your children, find out what they are doing and where they are going, meet their friends, and so forth. You must supervise what they watch on TV, the video games they play, and their use of the Internet. Access to guns must be restricted, and parental/adult supervision is required on occasions where a gun is used for sport. There is research that indicates that children who view aggressive behavior and violence are more likely to be aggressive than those who do not. While this is true, it does not mean that video games, movies, or TV programs are the main reasons for the aggressive behavior. A few other factors need to be considered when trying to predict the probability of aggressive behavior.

A history of violent or aggressive behavior would certainly increase the probability that this behavior would be seen in the future. The child's preoccupation or involvement with aggressive concerns or activities is another factor. The child who draws guns all the time or watches primarily violent movies, for example, would be more of a concern than a child who watches a variety of movies. How frequently this behavior is seen and how much this activity or interest consumes a part of the child's life are some pertinent questions. Another indication of potentially violent or aggressive behavior might be whether or not the teenager is part of a subculture or group that has ideas and values that are not consistent with mainstream thinking.

Although positive responses to some of the above questions will indicate an increase in the probability of aggressive behavior, some children who become aggressive toward other children in school do not have a history of violence or preoccupation with aggressive concerns. Instead they have had a tendency to be passive with poor self-esteem. Therefore, a person's personality factors must also be considered. Out of a caseload of about seventy children and teenagers referred by schools for psychological help because they said or did something with an aggressive intent ("I'm going to bring a gun to school and shoot Mrs. Jones," "I'm going to burn the school down." They drew a picture or wrote a poem or note that suggested they wanted to harm their classmates.), only two or three showed any real reason to be concerned.

Predicting behavior from personality factors is not a simple thing to do. It involves many components. Here are a few of the most important factors. Very generally, the teenagers to be most concerned about are the loners who do not have many friends and do not actively interact with their peers. These teenagers are excessively involved in many solitary activities (reading, watching TV, writing, computers, and so on) for their age. This is not the introverted, shy child who likes to read or write and who generally is conforming and seems well adjusted. The children to be concerned about lack assertiveness and the ability to openly compete or they lack confidence and are socially insecure. Compared to the shy, well-adjusted child, they seem to have a significant amount of underlying anger. When these characteristics appear with other factors, such as nonconformity, association with a marginal subculture, or unconventional thinking, a red flag goes up and, in some cases, intervention is necessary.

35

~~~~~~

WHAT TO DO IF THE TECHNIQUES IN THIS BOOK DO NOT WORK

If you have tried some of the suggestions in the book and they have not resulted in significant improvement, there are several things that should be considered.

Have You Changed Your Methods of Behavior Management? Remember, you are now dealing with an adolescent or a young adult and not a child. The type of control that was used with a small child will not necessarily work with the teenager. Compromise, listening and responding appropriately to the child's feelings, allowing her some freedom, and treating her more like an adult than a child should replace the methods that you used when she was younger.

Are You Still Reacting to or Becoming Upset with "Normal" Teenage Behavior? There are some typical changes that occur in the adolescent's behavior, attitude, and patterns of family interaction during this period. You must realize that the teenager is no longer the same child you used to know, but is changing and becoming more of an adult. Become familiar with the normal changes that occur and try to deal with them in an appropriate fashion.

Have You Increased Positive Communication? The adolescent is less talkative and communicates more infrequently with his parents than he did when he was younger. Therefore, the parents' interaction with their teenager often involves lectures, correction, trying to get a point across, and other similar communication. In general, the majority of interactions may become negative. If this is the case, the child may tune out the parents and not respond to their requests or suggestions. It is important to try to increase the amount of positive communication that you have with your child. Talk to him about his interests, the things that are important to him. Try to communicate just to communicate and not just to convey information or get a point across.

Are You Using Consequences Other Than Punishment? Punishment used as a primary method of control will not alter behavior in some children. In fact, it may make matters worse in some situations. The consequences of rewarding and ignoring behaviors must also be employed. The reward could involve loosening up restrictions on a child or giving him or her additional freedoms.

Are the Techniques Being Used Consistently? Another reason some techniques do not work is that they are not used consistently. Parents may try something one day and then the next day do something different. They do not stick with the same technique.

Inconsistency also occurs when parents use the technique but do not employ it every time they should. They may effectively deal with a behavior one time, let it slide the next four or five times, and then administer the consequence again the next time the behavior occurs. The techniques and consequences must be used consistently and should occur every time the behavior is seen.

Have You Given the Techniques a Chance to Work? Even if parents are consistent in using the same technique in disciplining, a method may not work simply because it has not been tried long enough. Behaviors in teenagers do not, as a rule, change overnight. For example, take a child who has been lax about homework since seventh grade, always needing constant prodding. Finally, by ninth grade her parents decide to set up a procedure to deal with this behavior. They follow a method very consistently, but after two weeks without improvement they discontinue the procedure. A behavior that has existed for several years will not disappear in a few weeks. Attempts to change the behavior must be tried for a reasonable period before they can be considered ineffective.

Did You Look for Small Improvements? A lot of the behaviors observed in teenagers can be viewed as habits or responses to the environment, which have gradually developed over a long period. When we look at our child's behavior, most of us observe the overall behavior. We forget to look for small improvements. You have to divide the behavior into small segments and watch for gradual improvement.

Are the Consequences Being Used Important to the Teenager? Whether negative or positive consequences are used, you have to be very sure that they are important to the adolescent. If the consequence used is not important or appropriate, it will not serve as a motivator and the behavior will not change. In determining a reward or a punishment, you have to consider the individual child's interests and values and use the consequences that are important to him. In addition, you must remember that teenagers are changing. What may be important this week may not serve as a motivator next week.

Did You Consistently Employ the Techniques if the Behavior at First Got Worse? Sometimes when an effective technique is being used, the behavior will get worse before it gets better. When parents see this happening, they may stop using the technique. However, the increase in this behavior may mean that the disciplinary tactic was working and the parent should not have given it up.

Did You Prevent the Child from Manipulating You? Children are good manipulators when it comes to getting out of being disciplined. For example, you may tell a teenager that she will lose her car privileges if she does not do her homework. When she replies, "So what? I'm not doing the homework. I didn't want to use the car anyway," you may think "What do I do now?" The child is starting to manipulate you. It may be true that she is not interested in using the car this weekend, but if using the car is an important activity to her and if you make this rule stick, the procedure will work and the homework will get done.

If the answer to some of the above questions is "no," you should use the technique again and try to eliminate the reason it did not work. If you feel that you have successfully implemented the techniques and you are still having problems, then it would be appropriate to contact a mental health professional who has some expertise in the area of adolescent behavior.

36

MEMOS FROM YOUR TEENAGER

1. Adolescence is a somewhat confusing time and I am experiencing many changes. Many of my behaviors are typical for teenagers. If you can understand some of these changes and can deal with me differently, we can both get through this period of my life without too much difficulty.

2. I am starting to change and I am not a child anymore. I am becoming a young adult. You will have difficulty "controlling" me the way you did when I was a young child. Try to deal with me the way you would treat your friends and other adults.

3. Opposition, resistance, stubbornness, rebellion, and striving for independence are a normal part of adolescence. Don't be upset if I disagree with you and begin expressing attitudes, interests, and opinions that are different from yours. Be more concerned about "how" I tell you things rather than "what" I say.

4. I have all your lectures on tape in case I want to hear them over and over again. Try to avoid repeating lectures, asking me the same questions many times, and nagging. If you do, I will have to protect myself by appearing deaf.

5. I will often feel that you are old-fashioned. You still live in the "olden days" when movies were fifteen cents, there were only three channels on the TV, and you had to walk twelve miles to get to school. I am tired of hearing "When I was your age." How could you ever understand me and know what is happening in my life?

6. Don't be upset if I do not talk to you or confide in you as much as I did when I was younger. This is typical for my age.

7. It seems as if your intelligence has decreased and, in fact, you're close to being stupid. How could you know what I'm supposed to do? How could I take your advice, directions, and suggestions? Bear with me. In a few years I will realize how much you've learned since I was a teenager.

8. As your intelligence decreases, my knowledge about the world and my intelligence increases. I am close to being a genius. I know just about everything there is to know. The only people who seem to be as smart as I am are my friends and peers.

9. I would rather be doing things with my friends than with you or the family. Don't become upset when I decline invitations to go out to eat, to go to Grandma's house, or to be with you.

10. You embarrass me and sometimes I don't want to be seen with you. I may stop bringing my friends to the house. You may have to drop me off a block from my friend's house or the movies so my peers will not see me with you. In the shopping center I may walk several feet in front of you or behind you so no one knows you are my parent.

11. We do not have as many chances to talk as we used to because I am always busy, with my friends, on the phone, or in my room. Because of this, most of our conversations center around my failures, mistakes, what I should do, what I didn't do, and other negative behaviors. During other discussions you're lecturing, trying to teach me something or get a point across ("the value of education," "what responsibility means"). Let's talk just to be talking. Try also to talk to me about my successes, accomplishments, achievements, interests, and activities.

12. It seems that little things you do irritate me. Even simple questions like, "How was your day?" may result in a flippant answer from me. Don't be too upset as I'm probably disturbed by something else and am taking it out on you. Moodiness is typical for my age.

13. Many times it may seem as if I have my priorities confused. This is not true. It's just that my friends, the opposite sex, talking on the phone, going out, having fun, and similar activities are more important than other things such as schoolwork, putting out the garbage, and cleaning my room. It is not that I am lazy; it is just that I have too many more important things to do than work.

14. At times it appears that you have developed amnesia. You don't remember what it's like being my age. You forget that you gave me the same lecture last Thursday, two weeks ago, or last month. You don't remember that you gave me the same instructions to clean my room or asked the same question "Did you study?" twenty times. You have forgotten how to shop and cook. There's never anything good to eat in the house, and I'd rather eat junk food than what you cook.

193

15. Don't become too upset when I mumble under my breath and complain when you ask me to do something—especially if I'm doing what you requested! I am angry at you for telling me to do something and this is a way to release some of this anger.

16. Don't use force with me or try to overpower me to get me to do what you want. This teaches me to be aggressive or resentful and gives me the message that power is all that counts. It will also make me more resistant, oppositional, and stubborn. This will probably result in my doing the opposite of what you request. I want to be treated more like an adult than a child.

17. Although I want to be treated like an adult, I will often act like a child. Rather than stress this, tell me what I have to do or not do to gain more adult privileges, responsibilities, and freedoms.

18. Avoid getting into power struggles with me. Power struggles usually result in a winner and a loser. You could win almost all the time when I was young. This might not be possible now. Set rules and consequences for my behavior and consistently enforce them in a calm, matter-of-fact manner. Try to compromise. That way we both win.

19. Try not to overreact to some things I say. Many times I am only saying things to get a rise out of you.

20. Although it may not seem like it, I need lots of understanding, encouragement, and positive attention. I cannot pat myself on the back, and I rely heavily upon you to do so.

21. Treat me the way you treat your friends; then I will be your friend, too. Remember, I learn more from a model than from a critic.

37

^^^

TIPS FOR TEENAGERS

1. When parents are unreasonable, don't try to reason with them. Smile and agree. It makes them think, feel embarrassed, maybe even guilty. Never walk away when they are talking. That makes them crazy.

2. When parents are reasonable—that is, when they give all kinds of reasons for a rule or decision—listen to them till they finish. Stay calm and then take each reason one at a time and tell why you disagree. They won't know how to deal with this because they expect you to interrupt, get angry, or be disrespectful. Of course, you have to have some pretty good reasons of your own or you're the unreasonable one.

3. If your parent denies your request or won't allow you more freedom, don't ask, "Why?" This will only get you another reason that supports the "no." Rather than "Why?" it is better to ask, "What can I do to get the privilege, request, or freedom?" The "What can I do?" question will give you some idea of what you have to do to get a "yes."

4. When parents get angry, it isn't the time to get angry back. A lot of times they're not upset with you but with their boss, the neighbor, or grocery costs. You just happen to be there at the wrong time. Look hurt.

*Some of these tips were taken from an article by Dolores Curran entitled "How to Get Along with Parents" (*Clarion Herald*, New Orleans, April 11, 1985).

Slump in your chair and look at them with pitiful eyes. If this doesn't work, get out of the way when they're in a bad mood. They need some time and space. Go outside, to a friend's house, or to your room. Eventually they will settle down and miss you.

5. Parents are unfair at times and this may make you angry. Don't discuss your complaints when either of you is angry or upset. Calm down and wait till they're in a good mood. Discuss your feelings later that day or in a few days.

6. When discussing your complaints, opinions, or requests, do not act sassy and flippant. Do not raise your voice; instead, discuss the matter in a normal tone. If you holler or appear flippant, they will hear only this. If you stay calm and talk, they may hear what you say.

7. Do not create situations where there is a winner and a loser. You're the child and will probably lose most of the time. How many times have you grounded your mother or taken away the phone privileges from your dad? Try to compromise and work out a situation where both of you win.

8. If you have trouble talking to your parents or if they get angry every time you try to discuss something, write a note. Put it on their pillow. Parents are pushovers for notes like this and will probably keep them forever.

9. Take your mom or dad out alone occasionally. Tell them you want just the two of you to go on a walk or out to eat. They'll be worried at first because they'll think you're going to tell them something terrible. Don't; just tell them you like having them all to yourself once in a while. They will probably cry or hug you. Put up with it.

10. Spend some time in the same room with your parents while they are watching TV or reading. Sit down and talk to them about school, your friends, or something else that interests you. At first they may think you're on some type of drug because of the change in your behavior. They'll get over this feeling and will love the "new you."

11. You do not do favors for people who argue with you or are uncooperative. If you act like this with your parents, there is a chance that they will not cooperate when you ask for favors: Can I sleep at Jason's house? Can I go to the football game? Can I use the car? Try to cooperate and minimize conflict because this will certainly work in your favor.

12. Ask your parents once a day, "Is there anything I can do for you?" Most of the time they will probably say no or give you something that will take a few minutes to complete. Your parents will love this and see you as a very cooperative person. When this occurs they will probably be more cooperative with you. You could also surprise them by doing something they don't make you do. They'll tell everyone you are the best possible son or daughter and, what's more, they will believe it.

13. When your parents are fighting, go away, even though you want to listen to them. Sooner or later they will get mad at you for listening if for nothing else.

14. Sometimes following stupid rules like turning off lights, cleaning up your room, or hanging up the towel after you shower may allow you to get some important concessions like staying out later, use of the car, or more phone time.

15. Be patient with your parents. Remember, they're going through a rough time in their lives and are trying to grow up, too. Help them to do it smoothly and with love and cooperation. Someday they will thank you.

QUESTIONS AND ANSWERS

I've tried everything to change my child's behavior but nothing works. What should I do now?

Much of the behavior observed in children can be viewed as habits or responses to the environment that have gradually developed over a long period of time. Your child didn't wake up one morning behaving as she does today. Her reactions to situations have appeared slowly and intensify with time. When you examine your child's behavior, you should look at overall behavior and for small improvements. Key 35 offers a comprehensive list of techniques to use when trying to change your child's behavior.

Some behaviors and attitudes are typical of the adolescent period and will be difficult to change. The teenager is constantly changing and becoming more of an adult. Become familiar with normal changes that occur and try to deal with them in an appropriate fashion.

I see TV commercials for psychiatric hospitals that talk about "Danger signals in teenagers." They claim that moodiness, change in personality, declining grades, spending more time in their room, withdrawal from family activities, etc., are things that should concern parents. I see many of the so-called "danger signals" in my teenager. What should I do?

Don't believe those commercials. A few years ago, professionals only considered hospitalization of an adolescent

199

in a psychiatric hospital appropriate when he was a danger to himself or others or when he was severely emotionally disturbed. Today, with the explosion in the number of psychiatric hospitals, the criteria for hospitalization have become too lenient. Adolescents are being hospitalized inappropriately for many other reasons often before any other form of outpatient treatment has been tried. Unfortunately, the criteria for deciding if an adolescent should be hospitalized are often restricted to the extent of your hospitalization insurance. Psychiatric hospitals are a big business and hospital beds must be filled to make money. Many use "scare advertising" to make you feel guilty or claim that common behaviors are distress signs indicating a need for hospitalization. Don't readily believe them. Become aware of typical teenage behavior. Get opinions regarding your child's behavior from mental health professionals not affiliated with hospitals.

At what age should I allow my child to get a driver's license, to remain home alone, start dating, etc.?

These kinds of questions concern the age at which your child will be responsible or mature enough to engage in particular activities. It is difficult to give a specific answer to these questions because each child is different and must be considered on an individual basis. Other factors besides age must be considered in arriving at the decision of when a teenager should be allowed to drive, date, and so on.

Maturity and a sense of responsibility don't always develop at the same age. An adolescent does not necessarily mature at fourteen, sixteen, or at eighteen. He does not acquire appropriate responsibility at a predetermined age. These behaviors are acquired through learning.

If your adolescent is not showing an appropriate level of maturity or responsibility for his age, he still has to learn them. In order to obtain the driver's license, etc., he must show appropriate behaviors that allow you to trust him. The things that can be done to help build a child's trustworthiness are discussed in the Keys on responsibility and trust.

My child has changed. As a teenager, he is not the same as when he was younger. What can I do to get my "old child" back?

You cannot get the "old child" back.

When a child becomes a young adult and strives for *independence,* a number of changes are typical. Parents must make corresponding changes to effectively relate, deal with, and interact with the growing child. Don't expect an adolescent to act as though he's still ten years old. Dealing with him appropriately minimizes problems and elicits some of the younger child's positive qualities.

My child used to go out to eat with us, watch TV with us, go to her Grandmother's house, and generally participate in family activities. Now she seems to avoid us, wants to be alone, and would rather be with her friends than with the family. What should I do?

Allow the child to grow. This behavior is typical of adolescents. Don't overreact. Continue to ask your child to participate in family activities or go places with you, but do not be offended if she chooses not to. At this age, she would rather be with her friends or on the phone than with her family. Forcing her to do otherwise only creates more resentment and further distances her from the family.

As a young child, my son always communicated with us. He would discuss what was happening in school and what his friends were doing, etc. Now it seems as if he only talks to us when he needs to. We do not know

what is happening in his life. How can we get him to communicate with us?

Many adolescents do not communicate with us the same way as they did when younger. So several things can be done to increase communication between you and your child.

Try to provide as many opportunities as possible to be physically together with your teenager. You must both be present before any communication can occur. Keys 18 through 20 will help you understand this new development in your relationship with your teenager and offer ways to encourage communication.

It seems as if everything I say irritates my daughter. I could ask her "How was your day?" and she responds with a nasty word or a flip answer. How do I deal with this kind of behavior?

Teenagers do not communicate with us as they did when they were younger. Avoid excessive questioning and do not pursue an issue if the child does not want to discuss it. The many changes in adolescents mean they are more likely to have "bad days" than the younger child and this may be the reason for negative reactions. Look at your response to your child and be sure you are not reacting to her in the same negative way she is responding to you.

My daughter acts as if I embarrass her. She won't bring her friends to the house. When we shop in the mall she walks in front of or behind me so she won't be seen with me. What should I do?

This is typical of adolescents and you should not be offended. We represent old values, ideas, dress, and methods of doing things. Usually if we do not make this a big issue, the adolescent understands us better and isn't so embarrassed.

Why does my daughter become so contradictory and stubborn when I confront her or when we get into a power struggle?

When children are younger, parents and children get into power struggles with a winner and a loser and we win most of the time. However, with young adults, the more you confront them, the more opposition and stubbornness you meet. You are not dealing with a child anymore; you are dealing with a young adult, and the techniques that you use must change. Deal with your teenager as you deal with your friends or the adults you work with. Avoid confrontations and power struggles where there is a winner and a loser, because you will no longer win much of the time.

I feel that my child and/or family would benefit from counseling but he does not want to go see a "shrink." What should I do?

Few teens are enthusiastic about counseling. If I only counseled teenagers who wanted to come see me, I would be unemployed. Many teenagers view counseling as a setting where adults gang up on them and make them conform to their parents' wishes. You get a tremendous amount of resistance from your child if you tell him the counseling is for his problem. Most teenagers do not feel that they have a problem and resist this approach. Shift the responsibility onto your shoulders and tell them you need help to deal with specific situations. Then, the counseling is viewed as an avenue for you to learn how to deal with your child.

The first time I meet with teenagers I try to put them at ease by telling them that I would rather be fishing than sitting in my office talking to them. Not that I do not like to talk to them, or that I have a bad job, don't like my job, or need my head shrunk. It simply means that I'd be much happier fishing

203

than working. Then I try to communicate to them that the purpose of our meeting is to identify changes in their lives to their situation. This could involve changes at school, with their parents, at home, with their friends, etc. It is much easier for teenagers to talk about the faults of parents and teachers than to talk about themselves. This is a good starting place. In addition, it conveys the idea that not all changes have to be made by them. The problems may exist elsewhere.

My child does not listen to what I say. I have to tell her 100 times to do something or get upset, scream, and holler before she pays attention to me and responds to what I've said. Can I get her to listen to me?

Children refusing to listen is a common problem for many parents. Inconsistency in your methods of dealing with your child's behavior can cause this. Some parents do not follow through with what they say, so children feel there is no reason to listen. Stick to your guns, say what you mean, mean what you say, and follow through with what you tell your child you are going to do. Deal with your child as you would deal with another adult. State what you expect and what the consequences will be and sit back and do whatever the child's behavior tells you to do. Avoid nagging, repeating instructions too many times, and hollering and screaming. The nagging results in more resentment and decreases the likelihood they will perform as we desire.

It seems if as if I am constantly battling my son. Everything is a fight. What can I do to stop this?

Adolescence is a period of time when your child develops some of your values and ideas. You have to select which battles you want to fight. That is, if you are struggling with your child over ten things, of which only three are really important, he may oppose you on all ten. If you reduce the battles down to the three important ones, you have a better chance of winning. For instance, one unimportant battle I recently witnessed involved an A-B student at an academically advanced school whose parents continually nagged him about homework and studying, even though he was very responsible and did everything he was supposed to do. Why fight this kind of battle if it is not a serious concern? A child's messy room, the way she dresses, the music a child listens to, and so on, usually fall into this unimportant category. Focus on the important things and deal with these. Another way to reduce battles is to avoid confrontation and power struggles.

My son talks back. He disagrees with my opinions and suggestions. Now he has a mind of his own. As a child he complied with what I said. What happened?

This behavior is typical and the content of conversations is less distressing than the manner in which options are expressed. Don't overreact to differences of opinion. Discuss his differences in a sane, adult fashion. He is becoming a young adult and independent thinking is to be expected.

How do I tell if my teenager's behavior is normal and typical or a matter of concern to me?

When trying to decide what is normal or what to expect from your child, weigh several factors and become familiar with the typical changes in teenagers.

How frequently does his worrisome behavior occur? All children are occasionally sassy and sometimes don't listen. But excessive surliness deviates from normal.

How does the behavior interfere with the child's ability to function? Most children do not like homework but will do it. If a child's behavior restricts or prevents functioning like an average child, it has to be considered abnormal.

How does the behavior interfere with others? Most children fight with their siblings. However, if this becomes a continual pattern it will disrupt the household. If the behavior significantly interferes with other people's routines, behaviors, and activities, it may deviate from the norm.

Still, you must allow for individual differences. Every child has a different personality. One child may be sensitive, another talkative, a third shy. In determining the normality of behavior, consider the individual. Also keep in mind family differences and expectations. Although you may expect your child to say "yes, ma'am" and "no, sir," another parent would consider this unreasonable.

Consult experts knowledgeable about child behavior. Teachers, coaches, dance instructors, and others who work with children are usually familiar with normal age-appropriate behavior. Although they may not be able to explain certain behaviors or ways for dealing with them, they can easily identify unusual actions that differ from those of the child's age group. Listen to these people.

If you still think your child's behavior differs from the norm, contact your child's doctor or a mental health professional who deals primarily with children and adolescents. She may be able to give you information or directions.

Why does my son value the opinions and suggestions of his friends more than mine? He rejects my advice, but takes it readily from his peers.

In the beginning, we have a tremendous influence over our young children, and their peers have relatively little. But somewhere around middle school our dominance decreases. Then, as the child approaches the end of middle school, the influence of peers rapidly grows until it far outweighs ours. This is a fairly typical pattern. Hopefully, in the preceding years you helped your child build a good moral foundation and instilled enduring values. Try not to overreact to outside influences and try to get your child involved with peers likely to have a good effect.

My daughter says she never does anything wrong. Can I get her to assume more responsibility for her actions?

See the Key on responsibility for broad guidelines on instilling responsibility. These techniques help the child who does not accept blame for mistakes and failures. In general, you should spell out rules and consequences ahead of time and put the responsibility for actions on the child's shoulders. Don't nag, remind, holler, or get excited but just sit back and do exactly what the child tells you to do. If the child's behavior brings reward, that's her accomplishment. If negative consequences ensue, that's also her decision.

If your child is manipulative and her excuses are designed to soften the consequences of her actions, do not allow this. Stop the manipulation. Check out her alibis so this behavior will no longer be effective. If the excuses work, they will continue. If not, they are likely to diminish.

GLOSSARY

Bribery means paying for illegal or inappropriate behavior. Fixing a traffic ticket usually involves bribery. Bribes differ from positive consequence or reward. For instance, we go to work because of the positive consequences, not because of bribes. Reward and positive consequences are effective methods of child management and should not be equated with bribes.

Consistency is saying what you mean, meaning what you say, and following through on what you've said. Don't say anything you can't or don't want to do. Do everything you say you are going to do. This is the foundation of effective behavior management. Without it, the techniques employed with the child probably will not work

Effective rules and consequences involve expectations and consequences stated before the rule is broken. Both the rule and the consequence of the child's behavior must be clearly spelled out. Although this cannot be done all of the time, it should be frequently implemented. Tell a child, "This is what I expect you to do and this is what is going to happen if you do it this way." This effective technique of behavior management develops responsibility.

Grandma's Rule is an effective way of setting rules and consequences. It simply states that "You do what I want and then I'll do what you want " or "You do what I want and then you can do what you want to do." Other examples: "Complete your homework and then you can talk on the phone." "You can't use the car until your room is cleaned."

Ignoring or no consequences involves withdrawing attention from a behavior, not following the behavior with a negative or positive result. This is an effective discipline method.

Intrinsic rewards are self-rewards or behavior performed because it feels good. Patting yourself on the back for a job well done or engaging in a behavior because you enjoy it are intrinsic rewards.

Material rewards are usually concrete or material things the child values such as baseball cards, a certain pair of tennis shoes, or a poster for her room.

Natural consequences are rule-setting techniques that apply natural or logical consequences following particular behaviors. If you do not eat, you go hungry. If you do not do the homework, you get a detention. This is an effective way to modify certain behaviors, but the natural consequences must be important to the child. For example, if a child does not care about clean clothes, the natural consequence of not putting his clothes in the dirty clothes basket and not having them washed will not be effective in modifying this behavior.

Physical punishment is spanking, hitting, and overpowering children. This ineffective punishment fails with the adolescent.

Punishment or negative consequences are what the child views as unenjoyable, including withdrawal of positive rewards.

Random discipline occurs when a parent states a rule or expectation for a child but does not set the consequence for behavior ahead of time. For example, the order "I don't want you to get any detentions this week" is too ambiguous. It doesn't warn what to expect. The expectation for proper behavior is stated beautifully but we wait until the rule is broken to determine the consequence. Disciplining a child this way makes effective child management difficult. It creates anger. The child does not feel responsible for what happens to him. Parents will feel guilty for what they have done or taken away from the child. Avoid this.

Response-cost punishment is an effective form of punishment built on a system in which the child is fined and/or loses privileges and activities as a result of behavior. "When you do something wrong it is going to cost you something" is the philosophy of this system.

Reward or positive consequences are anything important or enjoyable to the child, such as activities the child values. These include extra phone time, staying up past bedtime, having a friend sleep over. These could also involve activities that cost money such as renting a movie, ordering pizza, or going bowling.

Social rewards include praise, recognition, and positive attention for good behavior. These are the most powerful tools for reward parents possess and don't cost a penny. Social reward, positive attention, and nonverbal approval for good behavior are very important in behavior management.

Time-out punishment is an effective form of punishment that removes a child from an activity he enjoys. An example: while watching a favorite television program, a child aggravates his brother and is sent to his room.

Verbal punishment includes hollering, criticizing, name calling, and lecturing to make the child feel guilty, embarrassed, or fearful. This ineffective form of punishment should be avoided.

SUGGESTED READING

Aftab, Parry. *The Parent's Guide to Protecting Your Children in Cyberspace* (McGraw-Hill, 2000).

Arp, David and Claudia. *Suddenly They're 13: or the art of hugging a cactus* (Zondervan, 1999).

Bluestein, Jane. *Parents, Teens and Boundaries: How to Draw the Line* (Health Communications, 1993).

Elium, Jeanne and Don. *Raising a Teenager* (Celestial Arts, 1999).

Giannetti, Charlene C. and Sagarese, Margaret. *The Roller-Coaster Years: Raising Your Child Through the Maddening Yet Magical Middle School Years* (Broadway Books, 1997).

Nelson, Jane and Lott, Lynn. *I'm on Your Side: Resolving Conflict with Your Teenage Son or Daughter* (Prima, 1991).

Packer, Alex J. *Bringing Up Parents: The Teenager's Handbook* (Free Spirit, 1992).

Phelan, Thomas W. *Surviving Your Adolescents: How to Manage and Let Go of Your 13–18 Year Olds* (Child Management, 1998).

Pickhardt, Carl. *Keys to Raising a Drug-Free Child* (Barron's, 1999).

Rosenberg, Ellen. *Get a Clue!: A Parents' Guide to Understanding and Communicating with Your Preteen* (Owl Books, 1999).

Trace, F. and Felton, Louise. *Grounded for Life: Stop Blowing Your Fuse and Start Communicating* (Parenting Press, 1994).

Wolf, Anthony E. *Get Out of My Life, but First Could You Drive Me and Cheryl to the Mall?: A Parent's Guide to the New Teenager* (Noonday Press, 1992).

INDEX